# India, the Eter

## Mr. Bishnubrata Patra

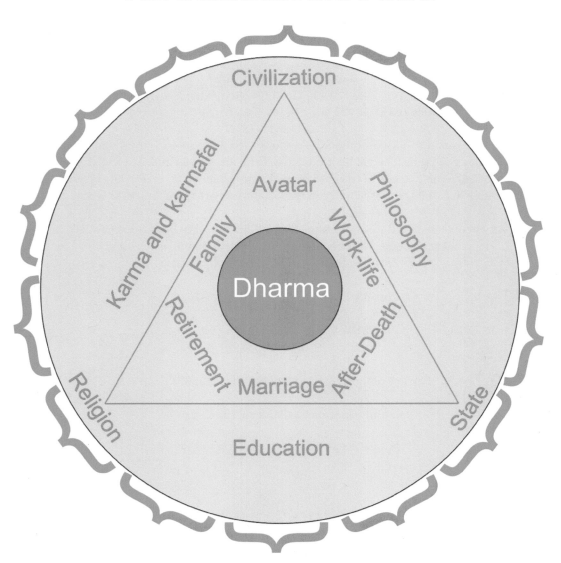

AuthorHouse™ UK
1663 Liberty Drive
Bloomington, IN 47403  USA
www.authorhouse.co.uk
UK TFN: 0800 0148641 (Toll Free inside the UK)
UK Local: 02036 956322 (+44 20 3695 6322 from outside the UK)

Because of the dynamic nature of the Internet, any web addresses or links contained in this book may have changed since publication and may no longer be valid. The views expressed in this work are solely those of the author and do not necessarily reflect the views of the publisher, and the publisher hereby disclaims any responsibility for them.

Any people depicted in stock imagery provided by Getty Images are models, and such images are being used for illustrative purposes only.
Certain stock imagery © Getty Images.

This book is printed on acid-free paper.

ISBN: 979-8-8230-8320-1 (sc)
ISBN: 979-8-8230-8319-5 (e)

Library of Congress Control Number: 2023911522

Print information available on the last page.

Published by AuthorHouse 07/11/2023

**author**HOUSE®

# CONTENTS

To my wife Manimala, my
parents, family, in-laws, relatives,
teachers, colleagues, friends,
and neighbors. I could never
write the book without them!

# PREFACE

*India before 15th August 1947, 11 British Indian provinces and more than 500 princely States*

# WE, THE PEOPLE!

Dear Readers,

Here is the map of the Indian Subcontinent before 1947. We can look at it from any direction. There is no right or wrong side to looking at it.

In this book, we will try to see many other things from different approaches. We will discuss the partition and independence of British India. We are going to make a plan/manifesto to build a caste-free society in the Subcontinent. We will study the countries and the States in the modern world to understand how the States in the Subcontinent can collaborate with each other towards mutual prosperity. Then, I would like to share some of my random thoughts with you. Finally, I will tell you how I came to write this book.

Before we start, it is important that we clearly understand who we are! Let me begin with myself. I am from India-Bharat. My mother tongue is Bengali. I live in Southampton, UK. I also have a name. However, these do not tell you enough. To know me, you would like to know a bit more. As a person, I can be a male, female or a third gender. According to belief, I can believe in a creator of this Universe, or I may not. I could feel that the Universe is the manifestation of that Absolute itself. Finally, I can accept that I am that Absolute! As for food habits, I can be a vegan, vegetarian as well as a non-vegetarian! However, most of these things I inherited from my parents or from my society or my belief. Then what is my identity?

The population of the world at present is almost eight billion. We all are Homo Sapiens! We can divide ourselves into three age groups: up to 22 years, 23-60 years, and more than 60 years old. The people who are 23-60 years old can be divided into four main groups according to their occupation (The figure: Identity system for modern society).

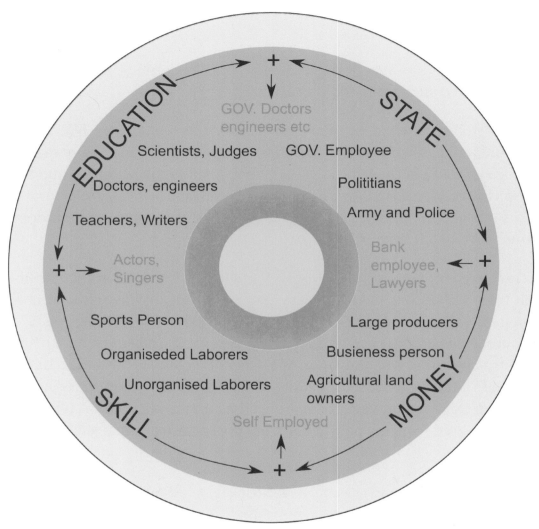

STUDENT

PROFESSIONAL

RETIREMENT

SEEK ENLIGHTENMENT

*Identity system for modern society. It is like a wheel rotating day and night! There is no any up or down side of that wheel.*

1. Some of us are directly employed by the State. They have a regular monthly salary and other benefits after retirement (**State**).
2. Some of us are employed in the education or knowledge sector and receive a monthly salary from the Government or a private employer **(Knowledge).**
3. Some of us earn our living by our skills, either as organized labourers or unorganized labourers. Some of us have monthly salaries, while others do not have a regular income **(Skill).**
4. Finally, some of us give employment to others, e.g., industrialists, businesspeople, agricultural landowners etc. Mostly, this forms the richest part of the society **(Money).**

Each main group (State, Money, Skill, Education) can be subdivided into three subgroups. There are some people who are in between two main groups, which also form four subgroups.

i) Government doctors, engineers, teachers etc. **(State and Knowledge).**
ii) Singers, actors, painters etc. **(Knowledge and Skill)**
iii) Small entrepreneur/ self-employed. **(Skill and Money)**
iv) Bank employees, lawyers, and Government Contractors. **(Money and State)**

So, altogether, we can divide our working people into 16 sub-groups under four main groups. Generally, people aged below 22 years are supposed to study or apprentice for some work. Above 60 years people are supposed to retire. There are some people who do not want to earn money or get married and seek enlightenment; they are known as monks or nuns.

Now, any of my readers can pin down what their identity is. They could also identify me. I am a researcher in a Biotech company in the UK.

I want to mention that,

1. I am not associated with any political organization.
2. I am not associated with any religious organization.
3. I am not associated with the socio-political organization.

Finally, I would request my readers not to translate my book into other languages. I hope you will enjoy reading it!

Bishnubrata Patra
(01/01/2023)

# BRITISH INDIA; PARTITION AND INDEPENDENCE

More than seventy years ago, the Indian Subcontinent started its new journey, breaking free from the bondage of the British Empire. However, partition came to be the inevitable outcome of that independence. Today, even after seventy years, it remains a question to many: "why was India partitioned?"

In this book, we will try to answer this question by understanding the history of that time and discussing some proposals to reunite the entire Indian subcontinent. Let us begin our journey by reminding ourselves of some key historical events that influenced the fate of the Indian subcontinent significantly.

# SOME OF THE HISTORICAL FACTS WE MIGHT HAVE FORGOTTEN:

1. British East India Company was formed around 1600 CE with a Royal Charter to do business with India and China.
2. Until 1700 CE, the British East India Company was doing exports and imports between Asia and Europe. Indian businesspeople earned great profits from their trades with the East India Company, which was one of the biggest exporters from India, along with other European companies of Dutch, French, Danish and Portuguese origins.
3. Onward 1707 CE, following the death of the Mughal emperor Aurangzeb, the main power centre of India shifted towards the south, albeit the Mughal rule remained in Delhi.
4. The British East India Company emerged as a political entity in 1757 at the battle of Palashi, Bengal.
5. Within one hundred years, the British East India Company gained control over most of the subcontinent, defeating Marathas in the south and Sikhs in the North. Then came the mutiny of 1857.
6. The mutiny of 1857 was mostly conducted by troops working under the East India Company and some princely states which were still not completely under the Company's rule. The mutiny was neither well organized nor had any proper motivation. However, some individuals made valiant contributions, Queen Lakshmibai being one of them!
7. Indian national movements started onwards 1905, opposing the partition of Bengal. However, the partition was revoked in 1911.
8. On April 8th, 1928, Mr Bhagat Singh and Mr Batukeshwar Dutta detonated a smoke bomb at the Central Legislative Assembly in

Delhi to protest against the newly imposed Trade Dispute Bill and the Public Safety Bill. The master mind behind the operation was Mr Chandrasekhar Azad. Although nobody suffered serious harm in the blast, a new chapter began in the history of the Indian freedom struggle. The political thoughts and plans of those who believed in the armed struggle came to light of public knowledge, and the idea of full self-governance or total independence began to be discussed among the masses. Certainly, they were not mere rebels against the British Government. Rather, they wanted to change the socio-economic structure of the country from the root. With the success of Bhagat Singh, the Lahore session of the "Indian National Congress" (1929) adopted the first "Purna-Swaraj" or "Total-independence" resolution.

9. The creator of the name "Pakistan" was an Indian student living in England, Choudhry Rahmat Ali. In 1933, Mr Ali proposed the name as an acronym for the combination of states in the north-western part of India; Punjab, Afgania (NWFP), Kashmir, Indus, Sindh, and Baluchistan. A notable fact is that Bengal was not included at all in the name of Pakistan. Initially, Mr Jinnah strongly opposed the idea of Pakistan as a separate State.

10. The idea of the Constituent Assembly of India was proposed in 1934 by Mr Manabendra Nath Roy (formerly Narendranath Bhattacharya), who was a founding member of the Communist Party of India.

11. Until 1937, Burma was a part of British India.

After the celebrated Salt March in 1930, Mr M. K. Gandhi gained huge popularity in India as well as abroad. Gandhi was invited to London for the Round Table Conference. During this time, the idea of separate electorate systems became more and more prominent in India to safeguard the identity of the minority from the number game of democratic elections. The 'majority' was called generals, and there were reservations for the 'minority' based on religion and caste. This was a good picture for almost the entire country. However, for the Northeast (Bengal) and Northwest parts of India (Punjab and Sindh), the generals were actually numerically inferior. Yet, no provision was made to protect the generals in Sindh, Punjab or Bengal. With the Government of India act 1935, general elections were held in eleven provinces in British India in the year 1936-37. However, the League failed severely to win even the reserved seats. Out of 1565 provincial seats all over the country, the League won only 105 seats. On the other hand, the National Congress secured 705 seats and formed governments in several provinces. The government of Punjab and Sindh was formed by the Unionist Party and the United Party. League was only able to form a coalition government with the Krishak Praja Party in Bengal. For more information, readers are requested to check the book Transfer Of Power in India written by V.P. Menon.

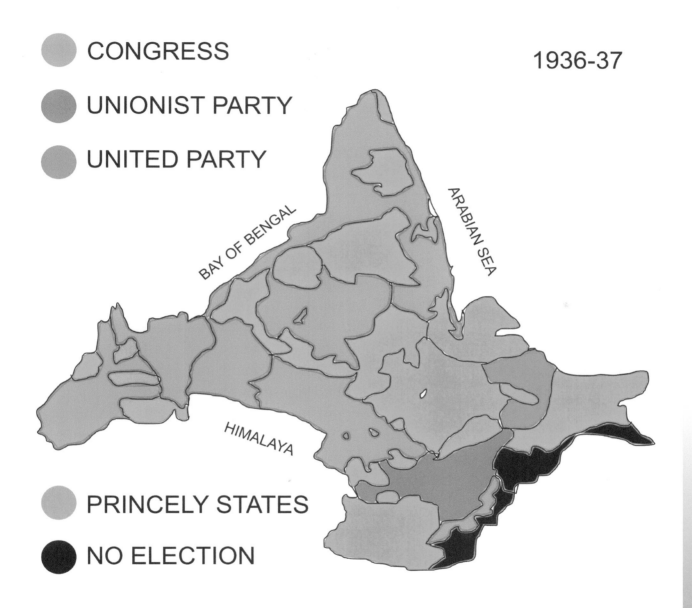

CONGRESS

UNIONIST PARTY

UNITED PARTY

1936-37

BAY OF BENGAL

ARABIAN SEA

HIMALAYA

PRINCELY STATES

NO ELECTION

*Results of Indian Provincial election 1936-37*

After the election defeat, the League realised that its power was not secured even in the separate electorate system based on caste and religion. So, League adopted a new strategy proclaiming that those who were not pro-League, were not genuinely religious.

Since 1939, the Second World War has been raging in Europe. By the summer of 1940, Poland, France and Northern Europe had fallen at the hand of Hitler. In the middle of 1941, amidst a strong fight in north Africa, Hitler attacked Russia. Two dramatic events occurred at the end of 1941. The German army was defeated for the first time in the battle of Moscow, and Japanese warplanes bombed the American naval base at Pearl harbour. By the middle of 1942, Japan conquered the Philippines, Singapore, Indonesia and Burma. The Second World War seemed to knock on the door of India on the Eastern Front. It was the time when the British government could not but seek help from Indian leadership to fight against imperial Japan. Sir Stafford Cripps, who served previously as the British ambassador to Russia, came to visit India with his offer of Indian Self Governance in return for support against Japan. However, Mr Gandhi rejected the Cripps Offer and started the Quit India movement on 9th August 1942. The British Indian government locked up almost all the Congress leaders. As expected, the League opposed the Quit India movement and agreed to collaborate with the government. As a result, League gained significant power among the provincial governments. In the meantime, League General Assembly in Lahore (1940) adopted a resolution to form a separate State named Pakistan from the north-western provinces of British India. It is notable that both resolutions from Congress [Complete Independence Resolution] and League [Pakistan Resolution] was passed in the city of Lahore.

By the summer of 1945, the war in Europe had ended. The great winner Mr Winston Churchill surprised the world by losing the general election in England held after ten years. The new Prime Minister was Mr Clement Attlee from the Labour Party. Congress leaders were freed from jail for the first time after the Quit India movement. In Asia, it seemed that the war would last at least two more years. However, the United States had something different in their mind. On July 16th 1945, The US tested the first atomic bomb in the desert of New Mexico. The US dropped two other bombs of a similar type on the city of Hiroshima and Nagasaki in Japan on the 6th and 9th of August. Japan surrendered to the US armed force headed by Douglas MacArthur on 15th August 1945. These events changed the political scenario in India dramatically. In September 1945, then Governor General of India, Viceroy Lord Wavell, invited Indian leadership to Shimla to discuss the future steps towards complete independence. Today, after 70 years, the events of the Shimla Conference have almost slipped from the minds of us Indians. The Shimla Conference failed to achieve its goals because Mr Jinnah, the one and only leader of the League, refused to include Maulana Abul kalam Azad (then president of the Congress party), Khan Abdul Ghaffar Khan (Congress Leader of NW frontier province) and Khijir Hayat Khan (the Premier of the province Punjab) in the Viceroy's council. This piece of information may come as a shock to many among us! To any common person, League must have been trying to safeguard the identity of a group of people considered as minority. But the Shimla Conference revealed that it was hardly the case! The definition of minority was determined by whether they were supporters of the League (a political party) or not!

After the failure of the Shimla Conference, central and provincial general elections were held again in all eleven provinces of British India. This time, League obtained unprecedented success, winning 429 seats out of 492 reserved provincial seats, emerging as the single largest party in Sindh, Punjab and Bengal. However, they could not secure a majority in any of the provinces! Although Congress won 923 provincial seats all over India, it did not do well in the reserved seats in most of the provinces. Again, Congress did achieve a good result in the Northwest frontier province and formed a government there. League formed coalition governments In Sindh and Bengal. However, the League government in Bengal was dependent on European representatives and the Caste Federation. Similarly, the government in Sindh was established by a very small majority. In Punjab, Khijir Hayat Khan became the Prime Minister again, and Congress, Akali Dal and Unionist Party jointly formed the government jointly. This is to say: despite the extraordinary success, the League was able to form governments only in two provinces; Sindh and Bengal, and those two League governments were likely to collapse any day!

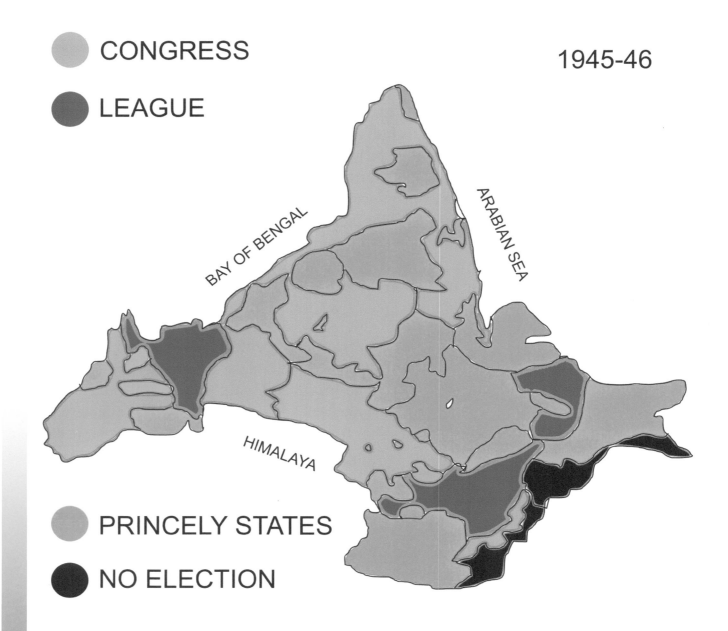

*Results of Indian Provincial election 1945-46.*

The Cabinet Mission arrived in India in March 1946. It was headed by Lord Pethick Lawrence, who was the then cabinet minister and the Secretary of State for India in the British Parliament. After consultation with League and Congress leadership, the mission representatives put forward a proposal. The proposal was that India would still be a single dominion, and an interim central government and central constituent assembly would be formed. The central government will mostly look after only four subjects: foreign relations, defence, finance, and communications (rail, air, mail). The provinces will be self-sufficient in other matters, including education, health, law and order etc. The provinces will be divided into three groups. Group A: United province, Central province, Odisha, Bihar, Bombay, and Madras. Group B; Sindh, Punjab, NWFP and Baluchistan. Group C; Bengal and Assam. However, the interpretation of the cabinet mission's proposal was completely different for the League and the Congress. The League considered the grouping of the provinces to be compulsory. On the other hand, grouping was a potential proposal to the Congress which would be finalised by the central constituent assembly. For more information, readers are requested to check the book India Wins Freedom written by Maulana Adul Kalam Azad.

Now, there remained the big question, who was going to lead the central government from the Indian side, i.e., to be the vice president of the dominion, just below the Governor General or the Viceroy? The obvious candidate seemed to be Maulana Abul Kalam Azad from Calcutta, the then president of the Congress party which had a majority in the central legislative assembly and was also set to be the majority in the future constituent assembly. However, Mr Azad chose to resign from the presidency of the Congress party, probably not to repeat the fiasco of the Shimla Conference in 1945. Provincial Congress presidents elected Mr Vallabhbhai Patel as the next All India president. Mr Patel too, withdrew his name after careful consideration. Finally, Mr Jawaharlal Nehru was selected as the next president of the Congress party. There were a few reasons behind this; firstly, Nehru was much younger than Patel in age, which could have helped to form a stable government until the next general election. Secondly, the vice president was simultaneously responsible for maintaining foreign policies and communications with the British Commonwealth (as a Foreign Minister together). Nehru's knowledge about foreign countries and ability to communicate in fluent English would have been beneficial in this regard. Finally, Mr Patel was particularly keen on the integration of the Indian princely states, which was to be executed under the Ministry of Home Affairs.

As the All-India president of the National Congress party, Nehru met journalists at a press conference in Bombay on July 10th, 1946. In his book 'Transfer of Power in India', V. P. Menon gives a detailed account of the press conference:

"Speaking at a press conference, Nehru admitted that in agreeing to go into the constituent assembly, the Congress had inevitably agreed to a certain process of going into it, that is, the election of candidates, but what we do there we are entirely and absolutely free to determine. Referring to the two provisions laid down by the mission, namely proper arrangements for the minorities and a treaty between India and England, he stressed that he would have no treaty with the British government if they sought to impose anything upon India; as for the minorities, it was it a domestic problem, and we shall no doubt succeed in solving it. We accept no outsider's interference in it, certainly not the British government's interference, and therefore these two limiting factors to the sovereignty of the constituent assembly are not accepted by us.

With regard to the question of grouping, Nehru said the big probability is, from any approach to the question, there will be no grouping. Obviously, Section a will decide against grouping. Speaking in bating language, there isn't a four to one chance of Northwest frontier province deciding against grouping. Then group B collapses. It is highly likely that Bengal and Assam will decide against grouping, Although I would like to say what the initial decision may be since it is evenly balanced. But I can say with every assurance and conviction that there is going to be finally no grouping there because Assam will not tolerate it under any circumstances whatever. Thus, you see, this grouping business approaching from any point of view does not get us on at all.

Dealing with the powers of the proposed union centre, Nehru Said defence and communications would embrace a large number of industries necessary for their support.

Foreign affairs must inevitably include foreign trade policy. It was equally inevitable that the union must raise its finances by taxation rather than by any system of contribution or doles from the provinces. Further, the centre must obviously control currency and credit, and there must be an overall authority to settle interprovincial disputes and to deal with administrative or economic breakdowns."

Let us now take a look into another description of that very same press conference from the book 'India wins freedom' written by Maulana Abul Kalam Azad.

"Now happened one of those unfortunate events which changed the course of history. On 10th July, Jawaharlal (Nehru) held a press conference in Bombay, "In which he made an astonishing statement. Some press representatives asked him, and with the passing of the resolution by the AICC, Congress had accepted the plan in toto including the competition with the interim government.

Jawarharlal, in reply, stated that Congress would enter the constituent assembly completely unfettered By and free to meet all situations as they arise. Press representatives further asked if this meant that the cabinet mission plan could be modified.

Jawarharlal replied emphatically that Congress had agreed only to participate Indian constituent assembly and regarded itself free to change or modify the cabinet mission plan as it thought based.

The Muslim League had accepted the cabinet mission plan only under duress. Naturally, Mr Jinnah was not very happy about it. In his speech to the League council, he had clearly stated he recommended acceptance only because nothing better could be obtained. His political adversities Started to criticise him by saying that he had failed to deliver the goods. They accused him that he had given off the idea of an independent Islamic state. If the league was willing to accept the cabinet mission plan, which denied the right of the Muslims to form a separate state, why had Mr Jinnah made so much fuss about an independent Islamic state?

Mr Jinnah was thus not at all happy about the outcome of the negotiation with the cabinet mission. Jawaharlal's statement came to him as a bombshell. He immediately issued a statement that this declaration by the Congress president demanded a review of the whole situation. He accordingly asked Liaquat Ali Khan to call a meeting of the league council, and he issued a statement to the following effect. The Muslim league council had accepted the cabinet mission plan as it was assured that the Congress also had accepted the scheme and the plan would be the basis of the future constitution of India. Now the Congress president had declared that the Congress could change the scheme through its majority in the constituent assembly; this would mean that the minorities would be placed at the mercy of the majority. His view was that Jawaharlal's declaration meant that Congress had rejected the cabinet mission plan, and such the viceroy should call upon the Muslim League, which had accepted the plan, to form the government.

The Muslim League council met in Bombay on 27 July. Mr Jinnah, in his opening speech, reiterated the demand for Pakistan as the only course left open to the Muslim league. After three days of discussion, the council passed a resolution rejecting the cabinet mission plan. It also decided to resort to direct action for the achievement of Pakistan."

"India wins freedom" is a much more popular book in the present Indian subcontinent compared to the book "Transfer of power in India." It is noticeable that Azad dedicated "India wins freedom" to Nehru as a friend and comrade. However, the book puts the entire blame for the failure of the Cabinet Mission plan on Nehru. In his view, if Patel had been the president of Congress, Jinnah could not have the opportunity to destroy the plan. As a result, Nehru was and continues to be much criticised in the educated society in Bangladesh, Pakistan as well as in India. However, if we read the account of V.P. Menon, then we find nothing incorrect in Nehru's answers.

1. The members of the newly formed constituent assembly should independently decide the future of the country, stressfully to the relationship between India and England.

2. No province can be compelled to join any group against the will of the provincial government or the elected representatives of that province, which means power sharing between the central government and the provincial governments. So, instead of a very strong centre, Nehru was in favour of the empowerment of the provincial governments.

Mr Nehru spoke like a secular democratic leader. But looking back after 75 years, it seems that it would have been wise of him to remain silent on those facts. The constituent assembly could be a more suitable place to discuss all those issues.

Nehru's press conference caused a great deal of frustration in the minds of the League leaders. They realised that numbers decided the game in a parliamentary democracy. Nevertheless, with half of the Congress representatives, League leadership aspired to gain more power than Congress. League leadership announced August 16th as the 'Direct Action Day' in Calcutta. This eventually became a grave communal problem over the course of the next few days. Surprisingly, the Communist Party of India supported the League in their demand of Pakistan. Some people say even Mr Jyoti Basu, the future chief minister of the Indian side, was present in the meeting of the direct-action day at the centre of the city of Calcutta. It is also important to mention that the Caste Federation did not withdraw support from the League government of Bengal even after the communal problem in Calcutta. Mr Jogendranath Mandal and Dr B. R. Ambedkar were two notable leaders of the Caste Federation. Mr Mandal was more popular among the masses of Bengal. However, Dr Ambedkar never managed to become a winning candidate in the parliamentary democracy.

Under these circumstances, the first interim central cabinet came to power in September 1946. All the members were representatives from the National Congress. Mr Nehru became the vice president. Around this time, Viceroy Wavell came to overview the situation in Calcutta. He realised that Congress must be included in the provincial government to restore some peace in the communally divided Bengal. He proposed the League be included in the central government in return for the Congress joining the provincial government of Bengal. Some ministers with Congress portfolios resigned from the central government, and League members joined their posts. Notable among the latter were Mr Liaquat Ali Khan, who joined as the finance minister and Mr Jogendranath Mandal as the law minister. Perhaps Mr Mandal was rewarded for standing firm behind the Bengal provincial government even after the Direct Action Day. In his resignation letter, Mr Mandal stated that he agreed to accept the offer only after consulting Dr Ambedkar, who was then present in London. Had India not been divided, Mr Mandal would have become the de facto chairman of the drafting committee of the constitution as the Minister of Law. However, Congress was not included in the Bengal government. After Bengal, Punjab was the next target for League, which was the single largest party after the 1946 election but not in the government yet.

Many people consider that it would have been better if, instead of the finance department, Congress had given the home ministry to the League. The argument from Congress was that the work of the finance ministry was mainly bureaucratic, while the Ministry of Home Affairs was responsible for the integration of the princely states. The first session of the central constituent assembly began on December 9th, 1946. None of the League representatives from the various provinces of India agreed to join the constituent assembly. Mr Jinnah, on the one hand, sought to make the grouping of the provinces compulsory such that League could be a majority in Groups B & C. On the other hand, by not joining the central constituent assembly, he tried to avoid working with in the Congress-majority assembly. He even threatened civil war if Pakistan's demands were not met.

Over time, with the power of the finance ministry in the union cabinet, the League leadership came to have the last word in policymaking. A group of finance ministry officials assisted the finance minister in that regard. The communal problems beginning on the Direct Action Day in August 1946 started to spread to Noakhali in East Bengal, then to Bihar in the month of October. Mr Gandhi visited Bihar in early November and announced his decision to go on a hunger strike unto death if peace was not restored in Bihar. We can look at Mr Gandhi's activity from two different viewpoints.

1.  Did Gandhi commit a hunger strike unto death at Noakhali?
2.  At least there was Gandhi, who chose to do a hunger strike unto death in Bihar.

And what was the League leadership doing after the communal clashes in Bihar? In his book, Maulana Azad wrote that the League leadership widely publicised the Bihar incident in Punjab and NW Frontier Province and launched a non-cooperation movement against the provincial government. Those movements were not peaceful, to say the least. In early March 1947, the disagreement between Congress and the League over the central budget reached a deadlock. The beginning of the end started in Lahore with the resignation of Mr Khijir Hayat Khan, the Prime Minister of Punjab. It is worth remembering that Mr Khan from the Unionist Party became Prime Minister in coalition with the Akalis and Congress. Congress was the major partner in that alliance, with 70 seats, whereas Akalis and the Unionist Party almost held an equal number of seats (20 each). However, the League was the single largest party in Punjab, with more seats than even Congress. What were the reasons behind Mr Khan's resignation? I cannot tell you the answer for sure. But the ones versed in the game of politics could guess that Mr Khan had started to realise that his own party members were already joining the League secretly, and his government became a minority in the assembly. Perhaps this was the moment the League had been waiting for all along. They had always wanted to form a government in Punjab and Bengal. From the League's point of view, they finally had justice. From the viewpoint of Congress, they had given League Bengal in addition to the position in the central government but no more. So martial law was imposed in the whole of Punjab. The then province of Punjab was composed of the majority of Punjab in present-day Pakistan and most of what is now Indian Punjab, Haryana, Himachal Pradesh and the central capital of Delhi. Among them, Delhi was of immense importance. Another crucial factor was that the majority of central army troops were recruited from Punjab. Apart from that, the cost of keeping such a large province under martial law for a very long period of time was huge. Also, the navel mutiny in Bombay in early 1946 reduced the reliance on the military. The Congress leadership sensed the worst of "a real civil war." Among the Congressmen, Mr Patel took the lead towards partition and independence. Mr Azad has expressed his dissatisfaction with Mr Patel in his book. However, he could have been a little thankful that Mr Patel tried to save the country from the worst communal violence.

In March 1947, another major development happened in Delhi; Viceroy Lord Wavell was replaced by Lord Mountbatten, and partition talk gathered pace. In April 1947, the Prime Minister of Bengal, Mr Suhrawardy, proposed a plan for an undivided united Bengal, which would have initiated a third constituent assembly in addition to India and Pakistan. Initially, Mr Jinnah agreed to the proposal. Mr Sharat Chandra Bose from Congress supported the proposal. However, Congress leadership, like Nehru and Patel, opposed the proposal. The most prominent opponent of the proposal was Mr Shyama Prasad Mukherjee from the party Mahasabha. Over time the talk between Bose and Suhrawardy failed. In the end, the League (as a party) also opposed the idea of Bengal as a third dominion.

From late March to early June 1947, Lord Mountbatten negotiated with both Congress and League, outlined the formation of two separate dominions with two separate constituent assemblies and union cabinets, and received the approval of the cabinet of England declaring that on August 15th, 1947, the responsibility will be handed over to the respective central governments/ constitute assemblies. This is called June 3rd plan. I cannot but say it was one of the worst dates in Indian history. The partition of Punjab and Bengal became inevitable. Four persons can be considered to be responsible for accepting the plan of the partition: Mountbatten, Patel, Nehru, and V. P. Menon. Jinnah, on the other hand, can be held responsible for the demand of Pakistan, with six entire provinces. By June 1947, the representatives of Bengal and Punjab decided to partition. Surprisingly none considered the partition of Sindh!

In July 1947, a referendum was held in two places. Sylhet, a district of Assam, decided to join the eastern part of Bengal and the constituent assembly of Pakistan. North-West Frontier Province, which had a provincial government of Congress, also agreed to join the constituent assembly of Pakistan. However, Sylhet's decision was mainly in favour of joining Bengal, leaving Assam. For NWFP, Mr Abdul Ghaffar Khan decided to boycott the referendum with a demand for an independent Pakhtunistan.

League representatives from the United province, Central province, Odisha, Bombay, Bihar and Madras agreed to join the constituent assembly session in Delhi on July 14th. On July 15, 1947, the House of Commons in England passed a bill on the independence of the Indian subcontinent. On the very next day, it was passed in the House of Lords. King George VI signed the bill on July 18th. On August 14th and 15th, Pakistan and India started their new journey as two separate dominions. Sir Cyril Radcliffe was given the task of dividing Bengal and Punjab. However, the border between the two newly found States was unknown before August 18th. Calcutta, the capital of Bengal, remained a part of India, and Lahore, the capital of Punjab, became a part of Pakistan. The new central capital of Pakistan was the city of Karachi in Sindh. Dhaka became the capital of East Bengal as well as East Pakistan. Delhi continued to be the central capital of India. Religion-based political representation was abolished in India. However, caste-based political representation is still present in India.

Initially, it was decided that Lord Mountbatten would be the caretaker Governor General of both the new dominions of India and Pakistan. However, on July 5th, 1947, Mr Liaqat Ali Khan wrote a letter to Lord Mountbatten requesting that Mr Jinnah be appointed as the Governor General of Pakistan. Eventually, Jinnah's lifelong political dream came to be true; he rose to a higher position of power than Patel, Nehru and Azad. On August 11[th,] at Pakistan's constituent assembly in Karachi, Mr Jinnah called for Pakistan to become a secular State! Mr Jinnah was not a very religious person in his personal life. Between 1942-1947 he resorted to extreme communal politics to win elections. In the end, he wanted to build Pakistan as a secular State. Notably, the composer of the first national anthem of Pakistan was Mr Jagannath Azad from Punjab.

Mr Jinnah was the supreme leader of the political party League. He was also the speaker of the constituent assembly of Pakistan as well as the Governor General of the State of Pakistan. Altogether, it seemed that Mr Jinnah had single-handedly obliged the Congress to accept the partition of India. But within a few days, Mr Jinnah realised his failure.

1. The major chunk of the central revenue of India came from two cities: Calcutta and Bombay. It was almost impossible to run the State of Pakistan with its central revenue.
2. His dearest colleagues, who fought alongside him for so long, had no enthusiasm for the constitution of Pakistan.

At this point again, Jinnah chose to utilize the anti-India sentiment among the Pakistanis to keep Pakistan united. His attention was drawn to the two princely states, Hyderabad and Kashmir. Of those, the revenue of Hyderabad was equivalent to the central revenue of Calcutta or Bombay. Before 1947, there was a small princely state called Junagarh in the present Indian state of Gujarat. After partition, the Nawab and Dewan of Junagarh wanted it to be a part of Pakistan. But the Indian Government send troops to protect the local people. Shortly afterwards, the problem in Kashmir began. In early 1948, Junagarh decided to join India through a referendum. Until September 1948, Hyderabad was not a part of either India or Pakistan, and Kashmir was fragmented between the two States. It was almost certain if a referendum was held in both places, it would turn in favour of India. However, Operation Polo was launched to integrate Hyderabad into India. On the other hand, many small princely states were integrated into Pakistan, and the democratic government of NWFP was dismissed by the central government of Pakistan.

After carefully analyzing the series of events leading to the partition, one comes to the conclusion that partition, which we have always mistakenly considered to be a religious issue, was nothing but a political problem. Surprisingly, most of the notable political figures of the time, like Jinnah, Ambedkar, Savarkar, Bhagat Singh and Nehru, were atheists in their personal lives. Indeed, the electoral success of the National Congress plunged other political parties into an existential crisis. Therefore, parties like the League, the Caste Federation, the Mahasabha and the Communist Party allied among themselves at different times to oppose the Congress in their struggle for survival. On the other hand, religious connections in the names of institutions like Aligarh University, Banaras University, and Presidency College's student dormitory in Calcutta etc., also gave birth to communalism among educated middle-class people. Even the playgrounds were not free from communalism. In this context, the three leading teams of Kolkata football can be mentioned. The provinces of British India were the outcome of colonial governance. Before the Constituent Assembly, it was necessary to integrate the native states and rearrange all the provinces entirely. For example, Punjab and Bengal could have been divided into two/three states (East and West Punjab, Nort Bengal+ Coochbehar, South Bengal, East Bengal +Sylhet+ Tripura).

Many people in the Indian subcontinent still wonder if it was possible to prevent the partition of India in any way. In this regard, a few key points come to mind:

1. The members of the constituent assembly should have been chosen via direct election (not via proportional representation).
2. League representatives should not have been allowed to attend the interim government ministry until they had joined the Constituent Assembly.
3. Mr Sarat Chandra Bose (then the leader of the Congress party in the central legislative assembly) could have been chosen to be the Vice-President in the interim Government instead of Mr Nehru after the controversial press conference.
4. League could have been offered the future ministry of external affairs instead of the finance ministry.
5. After the transfer of power, Mr Jinnah could have been promised the highest constitutional position, such as the Governor General or the President of India or the Speaker of the Constituent Assembly.

On a different note, it would have been much better if the two provinces, Punjab and Bengal, were divided and the borders disclosed at least six months before the Partition of India. The partition was a complex and sensitive issue. When discussing this, one must choose every word very carefully. Those who want to know more about the history of this time can read the mentioned references. Also noteworthy are Subhash Chandra Bose's "Indian Freedom Struggle" and Jawaharlal Nehru's "Discovery of India". Free PDFs of these books are available on the internet. These books are a must-read for anyone preparing for a government job Indian subcontinent. Finally, one must keep in mind that British rule served the Indians terribly in most aspects. But let us not forget a few people like Sir Pethick Lawrence and Clement Attlee, and Stafford Cripps. Notably, the citizens of Bangladesh, India and Pakistan residing in the UK, even temporarily, can still exercise their voting rights in the UK elections.

The partition is an event that none of us can deny today. But can we not leave the history behind and try to reunite the subcontinent in the future? Partition began on August 16th, 1947, in Calcutta and ended on December 16th, 1971, in Dhaka. Let the turn of the country start on August 16th, 2020. Everyone having some connection with Indian Subcontinent must take a significant responsibility in this regard.

1. Pakistan, Nepal, Bhutan, India/Bharat, Sri Lanka, and Bangladesh can participate together in the Olympics and Asian Games. The name can be "The Indian Subcontinent" or 'Subcontinent of India.'
2. The visa system can be reformed between countries (Both Travel visas and Work visas). Then things like NRC and CAA will become irrelevant.
3. Maybe one day we can move to a system of combined economy (like the European Union). In that case, the combined map of the States can be the symbol of the currency.

# A MANIFESTO TOWARDS CASTE FREE SOCIETY IN INDIA

India, a name glorified by the individuals like of Buddha and Gandhi, is the most fiercely criticized in the world for its social class and caste system. It seems very obvious to raise the question, "Why would a country discriminate among its own people, providing some with every privilege while others are left without even basic rights?" Moreover, the most intriguing question seems to be how this system could sustain over millennia in this country. Here, we try to understand the origin of such a system, how it got converted to its present form and the ways to modify it to strive towards a better society.

## WHAT IS THE CASTE OR JATI IN INDIA?

According to linguists, the word "Caste" originated from the Portuguese word "Casta", meaning race. Literally, the word Jati can be used to identify someone according to his/her birth. There are thousands of Jatis in India corresponding to the professions of its people. However, the word Caste (Jati/Jat) is used variously in India. One might identify oneself as a Brahmin by caste, whereas Brahmin was actually a Varna. Someone also might perceive themselves as a Rajput, which is a Jati under Kshatriya varna. Again, someone might feel that they are a Musalman, which is nothing but a religion. There are some castes attributed to the various tribes; their identity system is predominantly family/ethnicity-based. Altogether, the Government of India addresses its citizens into four categories:

1. Scheduled Castes
2. Scheduled Tribes
3. Other Backwards Castes
4. General Castes

Surprisingly, religion is a secondary identity in this case. If I may explain it to you, a man/woman of any caste can be of any religion. In terms of privileges, both Scheduled Castes and Scheduled Tribes have reservations in higher education, government jobs and political representations. People from the Other Backward Caste category get reservations in higher education and government jobs but not separate political representations. Finally, it is worth mentioning that almost all religious institutions follow family-based inheritance. That applies to a priest in a temple as well as an imam in a mosque.

Let us now summarize some popular hypotheses about the social history of India in which the caste system plays a significant role.

Hypothesis 1)
The social class system (Varna Vyavastha) evolved in India around 1000 BC when Aryans came to India. In that system, people were classified as Brahmin (intellectuals), Kshatriya (warriors), Vaishya (business people), and Shudra (workers).

Hypothesis 2)
The social class system gave birth to the caste system, that is, Jati Vyavastha. And Caste system gave birth to Untouchability.

Hypothesis 3)
Buddha was an opponent of Varna Vyavastha (Social Class system) and predominantly opposed Brahmins, as Buddha himself was a Kshatriya.

Hypothesis 4)
Many people who were untouchables embraced Islam as it came to India in the early 2nd millennium CE.

Though we list them as hypotheses, these are considered to be proven facts in most of the developed world. However, the question of the social life of India before the Aryans, i.e., before Varna Vyavastha, remains a much less-discussed topic. The most natural answer that immediately comes to mind is that it was the caste system already. We can consider it as a clan-based society. So, we can infer that the social class system and the caste system are two competing ideas. The hypothesis that one gave birth to another is not valid.

## A DIFFERENT APPROACH TO LOOKING INTO HISTORY:

In the social class system, there are four key words i) Brahmin, ii) Kshatriya, iii) Vaishya and iv) Shudra. To understand the Varna Vyavastha, one must analyze the origin and evolution of these words carefully. In any language, words are normally created to describe something as an adjective. With time, adjectives become proper nouns. It is highly possible that these four words did not originate at the same point in time. In many cases, words are generated as a pair, having opposite meanings or genders. My analysis is that the words Kshatriya and Vaishya together form a pair. Now, let us consider two more words, Sramana and Bhadra. They naturally form pairs with the words Brahmin and Shudra. Altogether, we get the following pairs.

i)    Sraman- Brahmin
ii)   Kshatriya- Vaishya
iii)  Shudra-Bhadra

## SRAMAN-BRAHMIN

It is well-known that the Brahmins and Sramans had competing ideas. The word Brahmin came from the word Brahman literally meaning the Absolute/Unchangeable. At the same time, the word Sraman is associated with the Buddhist, Jainist, Charbak, Ajibak etc traditions. The main difference between Brahmins and Sraman is that Brahmins accepted the creation and existence of the world, whereas the Sramans denied it. There were six different schools of philosophy developed by the Brahmins, Sankhya, Yoga, Nyaya, Vaiseshika, Mimamsa and Vedanta. On the other hand, the Sramans developed a few schools of philosophy like Charbak, Ajibak, Jainism, and Buddhism.

# KSHATRIYA- VAISHYA

In the present world, the words 'Kshatriya' and 'Vaishya' are translated as 'Warrior' and 'Businessperson'. However, if we try to understand the etymology of the two words, then it appears that the word 'Kshatriya' may have originated from the root word 'kshatra' and the word 'Vaishya' from 'Vishaya'. The closest meaning of the word kshatra is a tool required to dig the soil or a city secured with a water canal. It is also notable that in ancient India, a district was called a Vishaya. From those understanding, we can say a Kshatra was a big city, whereas a Vishaya was a relatively smaller city. For the timeline, we can say these words came to be in a time prior to Buddha (~500 BC), which is also called the period of 2nd urbanization in India. It seems natural that, with time, big cities became more prominent as military power centres. At the same time, small cities became the centres of business.

This is my understanding/opinion about the social situation of India around 1000 -500 BC. The rural populations could be subdivided into two belief systems Brahmins and Sramans. As the cities were established, two new demographic identities evolved, which are Kshatriya and Vaisya. The life of an individual could be divided into four stages, student life (Brahmacharya), married/professional life (Grihastha), retirement (vanaprastha) and some left family to seek enlightenment (Sannyasa) as the last stage of life.

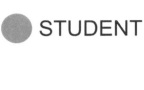 STUDENT

PROFESSIONAL

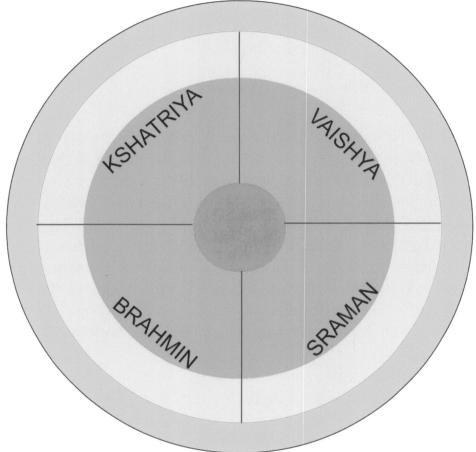

 RETIREMENT    SEEK ENLIGHTENMENT

*Identity system in the later Vedic period (~ 1000-500 BC.). Indian society was divided into four identities: Sraman, Brahman, Kshatriya, and Vaishya. Individual life was divided into four parts: Brahmacharya (student life), Grihastha (married and professional life), Vanaprastha (retirement) and Sannyasa (seeking enlightenment). The life of a person was a journey from the centre to the periphery.*

# SHUDRA AND BHADRA

The literal meaning of the word Bhadra is a decent/respectable person. The literal meaning of the word shudra is the very opposite of Bhadra. It is widely believed that Shudras were the non-Aryans living in India prior to the Aryans. However, this definition hardly bears any logic or proof. To understand the origin of the word shudra, we should analyze the economic situation of India between 1000 BCE and 500 BCE. Cities were growing up again at a fast pace. People migrated from villages to cities, the so-called Aryans and non-Aryans alike. However, there is always the possibility that the new migrants to the cities might not be well-adapted to urban life and got labelled as Shudras. The same tradition is still present today everywhere in the world. City dwellers normally bully newcomers from the villages.

# BUDDHA AND HIS DHAMMA

Buddha was born in a Kshatriya family. However, his family was engaged in cultivation as well. In modern times, it is popularly believed that Buddha started a revolution against the brahmins of the society. Historically thinking, there is no evidence that Varna Vyavastha was very strictly practised during the time of Buddha. Then what were the significant achievements that distinguished Buddha from the others? The answer is that he rejected the natural flow of the Ashramas. He was a married householder person, but he left his family to avoid going to war with his neighbouring kingdom. After enlightenment, Buddha started to preach his ideas. In his scheme of teaching, he tried to accommodate his followers in two categories; direct followers belonging to the order of monks called Bhikkhu/ Sannyasi and householders, Upasaka. The most significant change occurred in the "Sannyasa" part of the Ashramas. Previously, it was an optional final stage of a person's life. Now, it became an optional second stage, following Brahmacharya. The Vedic philosophy faced strong challenges from the Buddhists, as if Buddhism eclipsed the Vedas. In his final words, Buddha said all the component things in this world are temporary, which in turn developed the Buddhist philosophy; there is nothing absolute in this Universe.

# CASTE SYSTEM

The western world has long confused the caste system with the Varna Vyavastha. Direct translation from any Indian language reveals the names of the castes to be associated with various professions such as potter, blacksmith, weaver, fisherman, washerman, goldsmith, butcher, shoemaker, oil-maker etc. We can see that these castes are parts and parcels of city life. Caste is a larger family, including but not limited to the biological family, having the common factor of occupation. Naturally, the caste system became more and more prominent as the cities grew larger with time. Some of those castes were entrepreneurs, some were employed by others. Moreover, they came from either Brahmin or Sramanic rural populations. Some of them might have come from clan-based tribes as well.

## MANUSMRITI AND THE CHATURVARNA SYSTEM

Manusmriti is a book written on the basis of the four categories of the social class system (Chatur-varna Vyavastha) around 100 BC-100 CE. In this book, Brahmin, Kshatriya, Vaisya, and Shudra are considered as Varnas (social classes). Brahmins were teachers/intellectuals by profession. Kshatriyas were the protectors of people/ military persons. Vaisyas were businesspeople and farmers, and Shudras were household servants. The word Varna means colour; however, in this case, varna is used as an identity in terms of occupation. It is believed that the Chatur-varna system introduced a pyramidal structure in society in which Brahmins and Kshatriyas had higher social status than Vaisyas and Sudras. Again, Brahmins had higher social positions than Kshatriyas and Vaisyas were better placed than Shudras. Why was it so? Collectively Brahmins and Kshatriyas followed four stages of life (at least three stages) compared to Vaisya and Shudra. Kshatriyas and Vaisyas provided employment to the Shudras. On the other hand, a Brahmin could live their life without exploiting others and also could save themselves from being exploited. Brahmins were not very wealthy, even economically inferior to Shudras. However, Brahmins knew to live with minimum commodities. That is why brahmins were considered among the best of the four groups.

 STUDENT

PROFESSIONAL

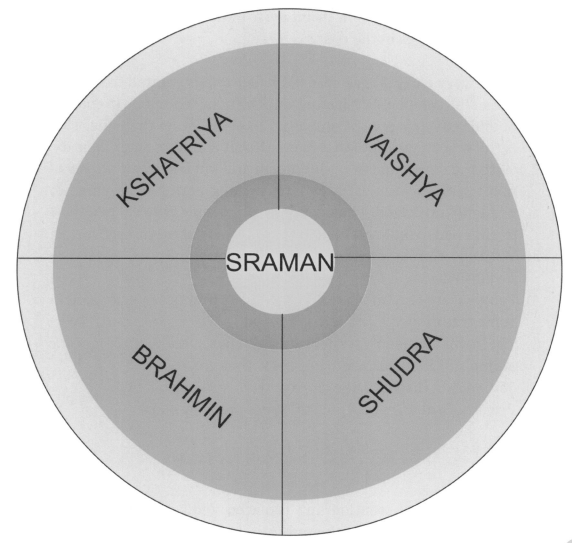

RETIREMENT  SEEK ENLIGHTENMENT

*Identity system in the first millennium CE*

# UNTOUCHABILITY

Untouchability is still a big problem in modern India. In my opinion, this problem has developed in different stages in the past.

1. In the very early stages, forest dweller tribes wanted to exclude urban life completely. Anyone from the tribe who came in contact outside the group was completely expelled from the tribe. This is the reason why Indian tribes can still maintain their identity.
2. With the development of Buddhism and Jainism, the practice of non-violence (Ahimsa) grew stricter and eating meat came to be highly criticized. Thus, the group of people who earned their livelihoods by killing animals lost their social privileges.
3. With the coming of Islam, the consumption of pork started to be vilified.
4. People were fearful of unusual religious practices performed in some traditions.
5. The nomadic people, especially the ones who kept dangerous animals like snakes, were kept at a distance.
6. Severe skin diseases like leprosy were still prevalent.
7. Priests (Brahmin) accepted all those steps by step.

## THE GITA AND SHANKARACHARYA

Buddha rejected the idea of creation and replaced Vedic rituals with meditations and control of the mind. In his religion, the only symbol was the Bodhi tree; however, with time, the country became full of holy relics of Buddha and Buddha himself was considered the Greatest (Bhagoaban/Bhagaba/ The saffron dressed). On the other hand, Bhagavad Gita is one of the most famous books in modern India. It is a part of the great Indian epic, the Mahabharata. However, it is highly believed that the Bhagavad Gita is written later. Surprisingly Krishna is addressed here as "Bhagaban." In this Book, Pandava warrior Arjuna, in a way very similar to Buddha, wishes not to fight for the sake of peace, and Krishna counters him. Social classes such as Brahmin (intellectuals), Kshatriya (fighters), Vaisya (businesspeople and agricultural community), and Shudra (skilled servants) are accepted here, yet there is no reference to ati-shudra or untouchables, and everyone is supposed to perform his particular duty selflessly (an individual is not important, the society is important). It was accepted that Shudras could acquire the highest knowledge as well. As Krishna, being the chariot driver, explains to Arjuna, Sanjaya, the chariot driver, explains Dhritarashtra the same. However, the intermixing of social classes (Varnas) was discouraged.

Islam came to India at its very beginning. The second Islamic mosque was built in 629 A.D. at Malabar Coast, modern-day Kerala. Perhaps its philosophy told that the "Absolute" or "Unchangeable" is the greatest. Maybe, with time, the idea of absolute was modified to a single creator without any form (monotheism). The Vedanta philosophy revived in India from the very same place, Kerala. Shankara, or Shankaracharya, was born in a Brahmin family in 788 A.D. He took sannyasa as if he followed Buddha. Perhaps, he received some assistance from the Uttar-Mimansa philosophy of Kumarilla Bhatta, and he developed his own thesis on "Brahma-sutra," "the principal Upanishads" and "the Gita," where he accepted the idea of Buddhist "Mayabad" as well. In his Advaita Vedanta philosophy (Non-dualistic philosophy), he said: all manifestations are nothing but absolute without any part; "Ayam-Atma Brahma: [Maha Bakya from the Upanishad]." In other words, there is no difference between the creator and the creation. After Shankaracharya, Buddhism lost its separate philosophical identity in India and started to mix with the rest of the people, which in turn influenced a large number of people and cultures.

# SUFISM

Sufism developed in Persia at the end of the eighth century and in the first half of the ninth century. It is a question to many whether Sufism is simply Islamic monotheism or it is a spiritual approach to Islam. Sir Md. Iqbal explained in his doctoral thesis, "Development of Metaphysics in Persia", that Sufism is an integration of Buddhism and Quranic teachings. It accepted the Buddhist idea of Nirvana as Fana, annihilation. On the other hand, the Quranic justification of Sufism was given in the following way. The Quran defines Muslims as "those who believe in the unseen, establish daily prayer, and spend out of what we have given them" [Quran, Sura 2. V. 3]. However, the question arises as to where the unseen is. The Quran replies that the unseen is your soul- "And in the earth, there are signs to those who believe, and in yourself,- what! Do you not then see". [Quran, Sura 51. V 20, 21.] Thus, Sufism developed a pantheistic view of the Universe with this Quranic justification, and the message to the individual was to love all and forget one's individuality. As also Rumi said: "To win other people's hearts is the greatest pilgrimage, and one heart is worth more than thousands of Kabahs; Kabah is a small cottage of Abraham, but the heart is the very home of God."

# POLITICAL CONQUEST OF INDIA AND ITS SOCIAL IMPACTS

Sufism and Islamic monotheism came to northern India with the political conquest at the end of the twelfth century. This was the time when the word "Hindu" became more prominent to describe the conquered political power. With the political conquest, the social order got a drastic change. The new rulers reached the top of the society, and Brahmins, who refused to cooperate with the change, crashed to the bottom. Buddhism finally met an end and was fragmented between Islam and Hinduism. Almost the entire Sannyasa part of Buddhism was taken into the Varna-ashrama fold, and the householders were divided into Islam and Varna-ashrama dharma. Where the Buddhists were the majority, they joined Islam. Otherwise, they were assimilated into the local population. It is highly believed that with the political conquest, Shudras and Ati-Shudras joined Islam in flocks. There must have been some of them, but if it were the situation, then there would be no Shudras left to count in India. After a few hundred years of turmoil, India settled again, and collaborative ideas could be found in northern India again. In the North-Western part, it was Sikhism, and in the North-Eastern and southern parts, Bhakti.

Guru Nanak (1469 A.D.) was born in Punjab at the end of the fifteenth century. His ideas were a combination of monotheism and Vedanta. He preached the idea of God as supreme, universal, all-powerful and formless, as well as that only God dwells in everyone. He also attacked the class and caste system. Guru Nanak's teachings are registered in the form of poetic hymns in the holy text of the "Guru Granth Sahib."

Shri Chaitanya was born in Bengal (1486 A.D.) in a Brahmin family at a similar time. He was prominent for the Vaishnava school of Bhakti yoga based on the Bhagavad Gita but with a dualistic approach as preached by Shri Madhava in Southern India before him. On the other hand, he took sannyasa like non-dualistic philosopher Shankaracharya. His message was that of love, "Naradiya Bhakti Sutra". His spiritual teaching made a substantial impact all over India.

The fall of Constantinople in 1453 A.D. marked the triumph of the Ottoman Empire. Within hundred years, the Mughal rule was established in India (1526 A.D.). Islam changed the social structure everywhere; however, in India, it achieved coexistence. Akbar the Great became the third Mughal emperor in 1556 A.D. He won the trust, as well as the loyalty of the Indians, by abolishing the sectarian tax on the non-Muslims and appointing them to high military and civil posts. India was predominantly an agricultural country, and for a farmer, the ox was the most valuable property. However, this was a movable property, hard to protect from theft, and if people ate beef, it became easier to hide the theft. Akbar restricted cow slaughter in his region, which in turn ensured economic progress. In his personal life, he assimilated the idea of pantheistic Sufi mysticism, Indian puranic beliefs and Jain vegetarianism altogether. Though Islam tells about a social class-free society, In Akbar's reign, as if Islam found a place in Indian society and one of the best verses of the Quran was followed: "Righteousness is not that you turn your faces toward the east or the west, but [true] righteousness is [in] one who believes in the Absolute/Unchangeable, the Last Day, the angels, the books, and the prophets and gives wealth, in spite of love for it, to relatives, orphans, the needy, the traveller, those who ask [for help], and for freeing enslaved people; [and who] establishes prayer and gives zakah; [those who] fulfil their promise when they promise; and [those who] are patient in poverty and hardship and during battle. Those are the ones who have been true, and it is those who are righteous" [The Quran: sura 2 verse 177].

# EAST INDIA COMPANY AND BRITISH INDIA

British East India Company started its journey as a political power in 1757 A.D. in Bengal. Within the first half of the nineteenth century, it gained direct or indirect control all over India. With the political change, new changes were expected in society. It is very significant to notice that East India Company, which was a business organization, got the top position in society. This was the time of interpreting Indian civilization with western views (Orientalism). Under the East India Company rule, Shudras and Ati-Shudras were given a mixed impact. On the one hand, they were crushed economically due to the industrial revolution and government policies. On the other, they were given some social freedoms by the colonizers. Jyoti Rao Phule was the first revolutionary thinker from the so-called unprivileged classes at that time. He played a significant role in women's upliftment and education, removal of social class and caste system and untouchability. This was the time when, after several centuries of struggle, Brahmins started to engage in occupations other than studying and teaching of the Vedas. Which, in turn, created more and more competition in society. The strongest oriental idea was to destroy the Sanskrit knowledge system. Towards that way, all the responsibilities for Indian problems were attributed to Brahmins.

Brahmo Samaj [1828 AD], Arya Samaj [1875], and Ramakrishna Mission[1897] are the most significant social reformers during the nineteenth century and early twentieth century. Among them, Ramakrishna Mission made and is still making a substantial impact all over India.

# GANDHI, AMBEDKAR, AND NEHRU

At the end of the British Raj, the idea of Buddha has spread far and wide. Gandhi took to non-violence, Dr Ambedkar took the fight against Manu Smriti, whereas Nehru, the atheist or agnostic, worked with the idea of economic socialism. Gandhi rejected the notion of caste (Jati), accepted the view of social class (varna), and firmly dismissed the idea of untouchability. Ambedkar, on the other hand, concluded that the root of caste-system are the Shastras (The Manusmriti) and rejected it altogether. In a bonfire in 1927, Ambedkar burnt the Manusmriti publicly.

Gandhi reached the triumph of popularity with the unprecedented success of the salt march in 1930 and was subsequently invited to London for the Round Table Conference. After the Round Table meeting, the British Government announced the communal award creating separate electorates for Muslims, Christians, Buddhists, Sikhs, and Untouchables. The award was strongly opposed by Gandhi, who was in Yerwada jail and fasted in protest against it. After a lengthy discussion, Gandhi reached an agreement with Ambedkar to have a single general electorate, with untouchables having more seats (142 seats instead of 71 out of 1565 provincial seats) reserved within it (Poona Pact). Gandhi and Nehru ensured the success of Congress in the upcoming election in 1937. However, the success scared others; perhaps the seed of the partition was sown at that time.

# AFTER INDEPENDENCE

Removal of untouchability was one of the major affirmative actions taken by the newly formed Indian constitution. The Government specified reservation in the Indian parliament was established for Scheduled Castes (SC/ Dalits) and Scheduled Tribes (ST). Today, out of 543 seats in present India's parliament, 84 (15.47%) are reserved for SCs and 47 (8.66%) for STs. Also, 15% and 7.5% of vacancies in the public sector and government-aided educational institutes are reserved for SC and ST candidates, respectively, as a quota. Later, another reserved category was generated for Other Backward castes (27%) in the public sector jobs (1990) and higher education (2006). Now, the society is divided into four parts, General Castes, Other Backward Castes, Scheduled Castes and Scheduled Tribes. The caste system is now maintained through reservations, not by the Manusmriti. The implication of the Mandal commission's observations [27 % reservations in government jobs for other backward castes] in the nineties (1990) caused a massive political crisis. No political party could oppose it directly. On the other hand, there was immense frustration among those belonging to the general category. It was the time when this frustration was channelized to another direction, and the religious difference became more prominent as a consequence.

# CASTE-FREE SOCIETY (ASHRAMA-VRITTI DHARMA), A GOAL

In the present time, the success of reservation is studied through a set of questions.

1. Is there a significant improvement for those who are getting reservations?
2. Is there a significant decrease in the efficiency of any organization after implementing the reservation in jobs?

However, we should also ask two more questions:

1. If there were no reservations, how would have been the society altogether?
2. If today onwards, there is no reservation, can the beneficiary of the reservation survive the open competition?

Justice, equality, liberty and fraternity are the ideas of modern nations. There should not be any undue privilege for anyone. Those who already got a caste-based reservation in education or job should deliberately join the General fold in the next generations. However, if we go towards a society free from any reservation, the difference between the wealthy and poor would be widened from time to time. So, we need a reservation for the weaker individuals of society to make a welfare state. Sportspeople should get reservations in higher education only. The idea of the Varna system should be changed to the "Vritti" (profession) system. The society is majorly divided into four professional groups Sramajibi (Labourers), Buddhijibi (Intellectuals), Rastrajibi (Statesmen), and Arthajibi (Merchants and Producers). Sanskrit knowledge is the real power of India. Strengthening our knowledge of Sanskrit will help us form a better society.

|  | **Definition** | **Restriction** | **Benefits** |
|---|---|---|---|
| **Student** | Anyone pursuing study | Cannot join any political party. | Free education and health care in government institute |
| **(1)Gov. Doctors, Engineers, Teachers and Researchers** | Anyone employed by Gov. according to knowledge. | Cannot do any other job, join a political party or possess agricultural land. | Salary, PF, Gratuity and pension (according to gov.) |
| **(2)Judiciary, Election commission and Media, CAG,** | Employed by Gov. or private organizations | Cannot do any other job, join a political party or possess agricultural land. | Salary, PF, Gratuity and pension (according to gov./income tax) |
| **(3)Doctors, Engineers** | Employed by private organizations | Cannot do any other job, join a political party or possess agricultural land. | Salary, PF, Gratuity and pension (according to income tax) |

| | Definition | Restriction | Benefits |
|---|---|---|---|
| **(4)Teachers, Researchers** | Employed by private organizations. | Cannot do any other job, join a political party or possess agricultural land. | Salary, PF, Gratuity and pension (according to income tax) |
| **(5) Actor, Singer, painter** | Employed by private organizations | Cannot do any other job, join a political party or possess agricultural land. | pension(according to income tax) |
| **(6)Sportsmen** | Employed by private organizations | Cannot do any other job, join a political party or possess agricultural land. | Reservation in higher education, pension(according to income tax) |

| | Definition | Restriction | Benefits |
|---|---|---|---|
| **(7) Organized labourers** | Employed by Gov. or private organizations | Cannot do any other job, join a political party or possess agricultural land. | pension(according to income tax) |
| **(8) Unorganized labourers** | Employed by private organizations | Cannot do any other job, join a political party or possess agricultural land. | pension(according to income tax) |
| **(9) Entrepreneur** | Anyone having some knowledge, skill, capital and self-employed with up to 9 partners | Cannot have more than nine employees or join any political party | pension(according to income tax) |
| **(10) Agricultural landowner** | Anyone completely depending on agricultural land | Cannot do any other job or join a political party | pension(according to income tax) |

|  | **Definition** | **Restriction** | **Benefits** |
|---|---|---|---|
| **(11) Businessperson** | Anyone doing business or products and employing less than 99 people | Cannot do any other job, join a political party or possess agricultural land. | pension(according to income tax) |
| **(12) Large producer** | Anyone doing business or product and employing more than 99 people | Cannot do any other job, join a political party or possess agricultural land. | pension(according to income tax) |
| **(13) Bank employee, Gov. Contractor, Stock exchange employee, Lawyers** | Employed by Gov. or private organization | Cannot do any other job, join a political party or possess agricultural land. | pension (according to income tax) |

|  | Definition | Restriction | Benefits |
|---|---|---|---|
| **(14) Army, Police and reserve forces** | employed by Gov | Cannot do any other job, join a political party or possess agricultural land. | Salary, PF, Gratuity, Pension, and benefits according to gov. |
| **(15)Politician** | Anyone completing education stands in the election at the local body poll with/without affiliation with a political party. The government would support the first three candidates for the next five years with the same salary as primary teachers. Onwards they could be promoted towards higher electoral polls | Cannot do any other job or possess agricultural land. | Salary, PF, Gratuity, Pension and benefits according to gov. |

|  | Definition | Restriction | Benefits |
|---|---|---|---|
| **(16) Government employee** | Administrative service | Can not do any other job, join a political party or possess agricultural land. | Salary, PF, Gratuity, Pension and benefits according to gov |
| **Monks and nuns** | Do not marry | Can not have a salary or Pension | **Free health care** |

*\*\*\*Two ashramas and sixteen Vritti systems, including all the population of the country. Joining a political party means being a member of the party or taking part in the election as a party member. Anyone can be a supporter of any political party. Anyone can change his/her profession(Vritti) but cannot continue two professions at the same time.*

## A NEW FORM OF THE RESERVATION SYSTEM

We should change society slowly but certainly. We should not stop the present caste-based reservation all of a sudden. But create a new reservation within the general category also. Students getting admitted to Government or Gov. sponsored schools (not privet schools) should be tracked according to their family conditions. After schooling, teachers should certify a student for reservation accordingly towards higher education. Similarly, colleges and universities (Gov. or Gov. sponsored only) should verify a student towards Gov. job reservations. With time, everyone should become General. Anyone who received Caste based reservations in one generation should be considered as general in the next generations. There should not be any reservation in Group D jobs; anyone doing Group D jobs should be considered as a priority (reservation) in other government-aided jobs as Group A, B, or C. For political reservations, the reserved seats should be shuffled in each election.

# INDIA AS A COUNTRY, BHARAT AS A STATE

Could you please tell me how many countries/states exist in the present world? There is no single answer to that question. In ordinary conversations, we consider a country and a State as equivalent. The United Nations recognizes 193 States as well as two observer States; Holy See and Palestine. FIFA recognizes almost 210 countries that take part in football. Again, 206 countries/States took part in the last 2021 Tokyo Olympics.

Let us take some examples to understand the problem. England, Scotland, Wales and Northern Ireland together make the United Kingdom or Great Britain. They represent themselves in the United Nations as the United Kingdom of Great Britain and Northern Ireland. They also take part in the Olympics Games together but participate separately in the football games. In this case, the United Kingdom is the State and England, Scotland, Wales, and Northern Ireland are countries. In this example, the State is larger than the individual countries. There are also opposite examples available where the country is larger than the States. The country China is composed of three States, the Peoples's Republic of China (PRC), Hong Kong (HKSAR), and Macau (MSAR). Even though Hong Kong and Macau are not members of the United Nations, they have their own passports and currency and take part in the Olympics Games separately.

Let us step back to contemplate our idea of a political State. A State is a temporary system having a particular territory, population, government, and sovereignty. In terms of sovereignty, we can think of military power, currency system and the power of authorizing a passport for its citizens. In simple words, when a group of people agrees to pay tax to a particular system and agrees to use a particular currency, then that system is called a State. In exchange, the State offers its citizens internal/external security, communications etc. On the other hand, the country is a geographical concept and thus timeless!

In the present situation, we consider the country and the State to be the same for India.

However, we can prepare a country named India, having States Pakistan, Nepal, Bhutan, Bharat, Maldives, Sri Lanka and Bangladesh. In the United Nations, States can represent themselves as,

1. India-Pakistan
2. India-Nepal
3. India-Bhutan
4. India-Bharat
5. India-Maldives
6. India-Sri Lanka
7. India-Bangladesh

This is no doubt a difficult task, but not impossible. To achieve this, we need to amend the Indian constitution. Presently, the constitution starts with "Name and Territory of the Union- (1) India that is Bharat shall be a Union of States." This needs to be replaced by "Name and Territory of the Union- (1) Bharat (The State) is a part of India (The Country) shall be a union of states (Provinces) and territories."

1. India can take part in the Olympics games together.
2. The visa process should be eased within the country.
3. In future, there will be a common currency system within India.

To achieve this, we have to understand the present status of the Indian subcontinent. Let us start with India-Bharat. Presently, India-Bharat is a State with 28 states/provinces and nine union territories. Bharat plays football as a team and takes part in the Olympics games. Even before its Independence, India-Bharat was a member of the United Nations (since 30th October 1945). After the partition and independence, the governing power came to the constituent assembly. After consulting all of its members, the constituent assembly accepted the constitution. The most important strength of this constitution is that it is not written by any individual/divine power, and it is amendable. Since 1950 (26th January) India-Bharat has been a sovereign-socialist democratic republic with a parliamentary system of government. In this system, the most powerful individual is the President of Bharat. However, the President consults the Prime Minister and the Central Cabinet before making any decision. The three main military forces (army, navy, and air force) wait for orders from the President. To make new laws or modify the existing laws; there are two houses in the central parliament. There are also the Supreme Court and central government employees to serve the nation.

For a province or a state, the most powerful individual is the Governor, who is employed by the President at the recommendation of the Central Cabinet. However, the state Governor should consult the Provincial Cabinet and the Chief Minister for every action taken. There are also state Legislative assemblies, police systems, state government employees, and state judiciary systems for the functioning of the state government. Regarding the local administration, there are city councils and village councils. This whole system was developed within 190 years of British administration. A significant part of the legislation was passed far away from India. Let us try to understand them step by step.

# GOV. OF INDIA ACT 1833

British East India Company was established in England during the reign of Elizabeth I in 1600 CE. For a century and a half, it was a business organization competing with other European counterparts. Those companies also had their armies. East India Company first got a political stake in India in 1757 at the battle of Palashi (Plassey) in Bengal. By 1833, the East India Company already controlled a major part of India, divided into three regions;

1. Bengal Presidency
2. Bombay Presidency
3. Madras Presidency

The three regions had their own capital cities, then Calcutta, Bombay and Madras. At present, these are known as Kolkata, Mumbai and Chennai. To control the activities of the East India Company in India, the parliament of England passed a bill in 1833 called Gov India Act 1833 or St. Helena Act. According to that act, the Governor General of Bengal was reassigned as the Governor General of India. By that act, India was put together as a State having three presidencies administrated by the East India Company. The rest of India was administrated by the princely states. The Act ended the function of East India Company as a business organization and made it a complete administrative body. That was the first legislation which approved Indians to be a part of the East India Company irrespective of religion. Calcutta Medical College was established in 1835 in the presence of Lord William Bentink, the then-Gov. General of India. By the middle of the nineteen century, three significant developments occurred in India.

1. In 1851, the first telegraph was used between Calcutta and Diamond Harbor (48 Km). By 1854, Calcutta was connected via telegraph to Agra to the north, Bombay to the west and Madras to the south.
2. The first passenger train ran between Bombay and Thane (34 Km) in 1853.
3. The Indian Postal system was developed in 1854.

This was the time when the British East India Company gained complete control over India. There were some princely states that had some understanding with the company.

The year 1857 could be remembered for two different sets of incidents.

1. Three Universities were established in Calcutta, Bombay and Madras.
2. The Sepoy Mutiny, or the Great Indian Rebellion of 1857, happened in north and central India.

The Sepoy Mutiny was not very successful in the end, and it did not have any major impact in most of the country. However, a few individuals made it eternal in history. Rani Lakshmi Bai, the queen of Jhansi, was one of them. She was and still is the face of the real valour of India.

# GOV. OF INDIA ACT 1858

After the mutiny, the Gov. of India Act 1858 was passed in England. The British East India Company was completely abolished. Queen Victoria of England/UK was empowered as Empress of India. All property and assets were transferred to the Crown. Now the administration of India followed a simpler hierarchy. On the top, Queen Victoria (As a symbolic head) and under the Queen, there was the parliament of the UK. The secretary of the State for India was a Cabinet Minister in the UK parliament. The Governor-general of India (Viceroy) was under the secretary of State for India.

# INDIAN COUNCILS ACT 1861

This was the time when Viceroy's executive council started to perform as a cabinet with five separate departments: Home, Revenue, Military, Finance, and Law. There were also some nominated members of the Council. The Calcutta high court was established in 1862 on July 1st. It was the oldest high court in India. Bombay and Madras high courts were established in the same year (August 14 and 15th).

# CALCUTTA TO LONDON

By the middle of the nineteenth century, two cities were the most important for the British Empire, London (the capital of the UK) and Calcutta (the capital of India). However, they were thousands of miles away from each other. By 1870, telegraphic communication was established between Calcutta and London. The Suez-canal was opened on November 17th, 1869. The fastest communication between Calcutta and London was a train to Bombay, then Bombay to Southampton via ship, and then Southampton to London via train. Otherwise, someone could take a break at Marseille, France, take a train to Calais, cross the English Channel to Dover by boat and finally, take a train to London. It took approximately 18 days to reach London from Calcutta, even in the early twentieth century.

## INDIAN COUNCIL ACT 1892

Indian National Congress was established in 1885 in Bombay. Within a few years, the Indian Council Act of 1892 was passed. The Governor Generals' executive committee was raised up to 16, and 2/5th of them were non-officials. The number of non-official members was extended in provincial councils also. The nominated members could ask questions of public interest. The year 1893 could be marked distinctly by the world religious conference in Chicago, USA, where Swami Vivekananda from India delivered an impressive public speech about Indian Philosophy. The reign of Queen Victoria lasted for more than half a century (1837-1901). After her death, Edward VII became the king and Emperor of the UK and India.

## INDIAN COUNCIL ACT 1909

The partition of Bengal was done in 1905, and the All-India Muslim League was formed in Dacca in 1906. The year 1907 could be marked as a milestone for modern industrialization in India; the steel plant based in Jamshedpur was established. Morley-Minto reform was passed in the British parliament to improve democratic activity in India. This was the first time elections were introduced, as well as a separate electorate system based on religion. The capital of India was transferred from Calcutta to Delhi in 1911 during the reign of Emperor George V.

# GOV. OF INDIA ACT 1919

Indian Poet Rabindranath Tagore (Thakur) received the Nobel Prize in literature in 1913. He was the first one from Asia to receive the Nobel Prize. In 1914, McMohun Line was drawn between British India and Tibet to demark the boundary between India and Tibet. In the west, the Durand line was there between India and Afghanistan since 1893. In the east, Burma was still included in India. Gov. of India Act 1919 was introduced to steer India towards self-governance. Two men who played major roles in this were Edwin Montegue (Secretary of States for India) and Lord Chelmsford (the Viceroy in India). The imperial legislative council was divided into two parts: the Central Legislative Assembly and the Council of State. More separate electorates were introduced at this point. Following the reforms, elections were held in India in 1923. Two major political groups were Swaraj Party (Motilal Nehru) and India Liberal Party (H. N. Kunzru). Regular elections were held every three years. By 1928, Simon's commission came to India to review the situation.

The Simon's Commission was opposed all over India. Bhagat Singh stood together with Lala Lajpat Rai in Lahore against the commission. After the unprecedented success of Mr Ghandhi in the Salt March in 1930, the whole situation changed dramatically. Mr Ghandhi was invited to London for the Round Table conference. On 16th August 1932, British Prime Minister Ramsay MacDonald announced the communal award. Other than the political development, the Reserve Bank of India (RBI) was established on 1st April 1935. The main idea of the RBI was presented by Dr B R Ambedkar to the Hilton Young Commission. The first civil aerodrome was established at Juhu (Bombay) in 1928 by J. R. D. Tata, the father of civil aviation in India. By 1933, Calcutta was connected to London via Imperial Airways, which was later merged with British Airways. The air connection continued till 2009. Presently, Kolkata does not have any direct air connection to Europe or the UK.

# GOV. OF INDIA ACT 1935

Gov. of India Act 1935 was one of the last few milestones of the British administration in India. Burma was separated from India by this act. The Federation of India consisted of 11 provinces (NWFP, Punjab, Sindh, Bombay, Madras, Central Province, United Province, Bihar, Orissa, Bengal, and Assam) and more than 500 princely states. The diarchy was ended in the central legislative assembly. The election was held in 1936-1937, with 35 million people, and provincial governments were established in all 11 provinces. The federal court was established over the high courts (1937), which later transformed into the Supreme Court in 1950. Onward 1937, war broke out between China and Japan, and by 1939 in Europe. By the end of 1941, Japan attacked the US naval base Pearl Harbor in the Pacific Ocean. So, it became another World War. In the meantime, Sir Stafford Cripps came to India. However, Mr Gandhi rejected Cripp's offer and started the Quit India movement (August 1942). The details of the situation can be found in the book 'India Wins Freedom' written by M. A. K. Azad. It is important to mention the visit of Mr Chiang Kai-shek and his wife to India (February 1942). Let us read some parts describing the visit from "India Wins Freedom."

"The Generalissimo (Mr Chiang Kai-shek) again said that so far as India was concerned, his view was that there was no substantial difference between dominion status and complete independence. He dwelt at length on this point and said that if the British Government offered self-governance with dominion status, India would be wise in accepting it. He added that he knew that Jawaharlal did not agree with his view and wanted complete independence, but as a well-wisher of India, his advice would be that we should not reject such an offer. Jawaharlal spoke to me in Urdu and said that as the Congress president, it was for me (Azad) to reply to the question. I told Generalissimo that if the British Government offered dominion status and agreed that during the war, Indian representatives could work with a sense of freedom and responsibility, the congress would not refuge the offer. At this stage, Madam Chiang Kai-shek joined us and invited us for tea. Her presence made discussion easier as she was trained in the United States and spoke English with perfect ease."

The Quit India movement in August 1942 was one of the very successful mass movements till today. However, people had to pay back very soon; in 1943, the Bengal famine took almost 3 million lives. If we look back at it after 75 years, it seems that India might not have been divided if Mr Gandhi had accepted Cripps' Offer. We might know that the Mahasabha and the League opposed the Quit India movement. Do we know the role of the Communist Party or the Caste Federation in reaction to the Quit India movement? It is also important to mention that Dr Shyamaprasad Mukherjee resigned from the Ministry of Bengal government, opposing the government's reaction to the Quit India movement.

## THE CONSTITUENT ASSEMBLY 1946

The constituent assembly was supposed to start functioning by the middle of 1946. However, there were three major flaws in the constituent assembly.

1. The election done in 1945/46 was still a partial democracy. Only a portion of the population was granted voting rights.
2. There was nominal democracy in the princely states.
3. The constituent assembly itself was a proportional representation of the provincial election 1945/46. That means the members of the constituent assembly were selected by the MLAs, not directly by the people.

The members of the League rejected sending their representatives to the constituent assembly, which represented approximately one-fourth of the population distributed all over India. Surprisingly, League representatives joined the interim central government! In my opinion, if the constituent assembly members were selected directly by the people, then Government could have done reelection if some members refused to join the assembly. Finally, this is also the answer to the question, "Why was India partitioned in 1947?" asked at the beginning of this book; A political party led by Mr Jinnah rejected to join the constituent assembly. There was no connection to religious belief or faith! It was a complete political problem. At the same time, religious and political leaders like Mr Gandhi or Mr Azad were running away from power politics.

# THE SUBCONTINENT AFTER INDEPENDENCE

Pakistan was divided into two separate political States within 30 years of independence! Within 50 years of separation, Bangladesh is showing much more promise compared to Pakistan. In future, it might be the most economically prosperous region in the Indian subcontinent. However, from Pakistan to Bangladesh or Nepal to Sri Lanka, political and social problems look very similar. Let us list them one by one.

Political problems:

1. Theoretically, all of the States feature multiparty democracy. However, in Pakistan, Army plays a very significant role in running the country, and no prime minister has yet completed the five years term. Presently Bangladesh is almost a single-party democracy.
2. Political parties take part in a democratic election. However, nowhere in the subcontinent do political parties follow a real democratic election to elect the party officials.
3. Candidates use the symbol of the corresponding political parties in the democratic elections.
4. There is no scrutiny of the funding of the political parties as well as no audit is done of their expenditure.
5. There are no eligibility criteria (educational / experience/ domicile) to stand in a political election.
6. There is no term limit for an MP, MLA or Cabinet ministers.

7. All the top political positions, i.e., the President, Prime Minister, and Chief Minister, are selected through a secondary election.

Social problems:

1. Conventional agriculture is no more profitable as a full-time job. People are rushing towards the city.
2. Renting or buying a property is not systematic. Most of the laws are partial to the tenants, which makes the situation more difficult to find a house to rent for the lower middle-income group.
3. The judiciary is very expensive, and there is no system for solving micro-scale disputes/problems. These are the problems within a family or among the neighbours.
4. Butchers, Shoemakers, and Cleaners are disrespected throughout the country.
5. Only a few people pay direct taxes, yet no particular benefit exists for those who pay them.
6. The army is considered a hero always. However, the social status of police personnel is poor.
7. There is no rational language policy anywhere in the subcontinent. Higher-educated people are comfortable with English. People with vernacular always stay behind.
8. Basic public health and education need much more improvement.
9. A significant number of people live their whole lives with the wrong date of birth. A significant number of people are assigned the wrong death certificate to claim government benefits.

# TO SOLVE THE PROBLEMS

To solve those problems, we start with two approaches. One is top-down; another is bottom-up.

1. To make India a better country, having multiple States.
2. To make Bharat a better political State.

Only better legislation can solve our social problems.

## TO MAKE INDIA A BETTER COUNTRY, HAVING MULTIPLE STATES.

Let us define our proposed India one more time. India is a country made up of seven political States: Pakistan, Nepal, Bhutan, Bharat, Maldives, Sri Lanka, and Bangladesh. Geographically, our neighbours are Iran, Afghanistan, Tajikistan, Xinjiang, Tibet, Myanmar, and Thailand. India should join the Olympic games together. The Olympics organizations of the subcontinent will remain independent entities. The Olympic Association of Indian Subcontinent (OAIS) is to be formed. A governing body is to be formed with the presidents of the existing Olympics associations. Every meeting will be presided over by a chairperson having rotations from the representatives. The first chairperson should be the representative from the Maldives. A headquarter for the OAIS is to be set up in Bengaluru, which is the most modern city in the partner States.

# There is no problem with the individual participants. Everyone who qualifies for the Olympics will be supported by the OAIS.

#For the team games like hockey and football, an internal tournament will be arranged to find the best manager/coach. The winning coach will choose his team and the support staff.

#The OAIS governing body will decide the official dress of the participants.

#For the anthem, I propose the song "Sare Jahaan se Achha", written by Mr Iqbal.

#The official greetings to be "Chak de India."

#For the Flag, I propose this one. The purpose of the flag is to include all the human beings on the planet.

*The Flag: Santi-Sambridhi-Sampriti Chakra meaning Peace-Prosperity-and Harmony of all humanity.*

To improve the diplomatic relations between the partner States, I propose a committee to be formed with the foreign secretaries (not the ministers) from all the States within India. The main ideas and goals are listed here.

#To improve the relations between the partner States and with the world.

#Improve the rights of movement of individuals within the partner States. Presently, Pakistani citizens can enter Bharat only through Mumbai and New Delhi Airports. These types of restrictions should be removed.

#Any restriction regarding the work visa should be removed.

#Any citizen within the partner States should be allowed a visa on arrival if they agree to be tracked through a mobile signal.

#The committee will have monthly meetings to discuss the issues.

#Two possible venues for the meetings are Kolkata and Lahore.

#Every meeting will be presided over by a chairman having rotations from the representatives. The first chairperson should be a representative from Sri Lanka.

#The partner States will agree on the Cartographic representation of each State. Clearly defining the area already under control and the area they claim.

#The partner States will allow dual citizenship within India as well as within the Commonwealth. The descendants from any partner States will be given priority in this process.

#The partner States will discuss the river water sharing among themselves.

To improve the economic cooperation between the partner States, a committee is to be formed with the Governors of the central banks of the partner States. Monthly meetings are to be held in a similar manner. Possible venues for the meetings are Karachi, Mumbai and Chittagong. The first meeting is to be presided over by the representative of Bhutan. The main goals are listed here.

#Individual citizens from the partner States should be allowed to exchange money without purchasing other foreign currencies.

#Easier bank transfer is to be established.

#A common currency system is to be established by 2047.

#The emblem on the currency should be the Taz Mahal and the combined map of the partner States, with Sri Lanka on the top and the Himalayas at the bottom.

# TO MAKE BHARAT A BETTER STATE

Let me present my proposals from the point of view of a common citizen of Bharat. I come from a small town named Kamarhati in, north of Kolkata, West Bengal. Kamarhati has been a municipality since 1899. It is also a constituency in the West Bengal legislative assembly. It belongs to the Dum Dum constituency in the central parliament of Bharat. It has three rail stations and two metro stations, several private/public hospitals, schools, post offices, markets, shopping malls etc. In terms of local representatives, Kamarhati municipality has 35 wards, having 35 councillors over 213 polling booths. In my opinion, each booth should have one councillor who should be a resident as well as a voter of that booth. The councillors should choose the chairperson and deputy chair of the municipality. Any councillor of the Kamarhati municipality having more than ten years of experience can contest to be the MLA of the Kamarhati constituency. However, being an MLA, they cannot have another income apart from the MLA salary. The chief minister of West Bengal should be chosen by the people directly. Any individual should not be a chief minister for more than ten years. No one should be an MLA for more than 20 years. For the parliamentary constituency (for example, Dum Dum), any MLA having ten years of experience can contest the election. No one should be a member of the parliament for more than 20 years. For any election, individuals must contest with their own symbols. Most preferably, it can be a numerical number between one to nine hundred ninety-nine. The reserved seats for SC and STs should be recirculated; the same seats should not be reserved forever. In normal situations, the Governor of a state is to be chosen by the state government/cabinet. During an internal/external emergency, the central government should send their representative as a Governor. The President of the Union should be chosen by indirect election by the MLAs and MPs. However, anyone contesting to be the President of the union should have at least five years of experience being the governor of any state.

# THE 2024 PARLIAMENT ELECTION IN BHARAT

Within one year, the State of Bharat is going to have its parliamentary election. Presently, the Bharatiya Janata Party (BJP/Peoples Party of Bharat) has had a clear majority for the last nine years. It is worth mentioning that Pakistan and Bangladesh also have political parties with similar names, the Peoples Party of Pakistan and the Awami League. On the other hand, Bharat has the opposition as Indian National Congress. As Bharat approaches the parliamentary election, obvious turmoil has started all over the State. The ruling party BJP has some agendas fulfilled in the last five/ten years,

1. Removing the Triple Talaque.
2. Removing article 370 in the state of Jammu and Kashmir.
3. Establishing the Ram Mandir at Ayodhya.
4. The make-in-India projects.

5. Improving the rail and road infrastructures, Bande Bharat trains are running.
6. Bharat is achieving more medals in the Olympics.
7. The government has introduced a new education policy.
8. The nation is not ready for agricultural reform, but the government tried that.

On the other hand, the opposition is complaining that,

1. There have been many bank scams in the last few years
2. The note ban was not successful
3. The GST was implemented poorly
4. BJP does not follow people's mandate in state/provincial elections
5. BJP is destroying the plurality of Bharat State.
6. Not enough funding for science, education, and research
7. Finally, Mr Modi is arrogant!

No one should not be a prime minister for more than ten years! But the question is, who is going to replace Mr Modi? We have to find the answer democratically. To choose the next Prime Minister of Bharat, we have to set some ground rules for politics.

1. No one should be Prime Minister for more than ten years; that is two complete terms of the parliament.
2. No one should be an MP for more than 20 years.
3. Anyone can contest in the 2024 election, but only in the constituency where they are a resident as well as a voter. It will be better if the candidates have some prior experience of being MLAs.
4. Candidates should have their own electoral symbols. Possibly a numerical number within 1-999. It should be randomly chosen by the election commission.

5. Anyone who becomes an MP cannot have any other source of income than the MP salary until the end of the Parliamentary term. If there is some other income, MPs should donate it to the government.

6. After the parliament is formed, the MPs will take the parliamentary oath and choose a speaker for the assembly. Any member can contest for the speaker post.

7. Within six months, there will be a general election for the Prime Minister post. Any present MP having five years of prior experience being an MP can contest for the Prime Minister post. Until that, a caretaker government will run the country.

8. The directly elected prime minister will choose the cabinet.

9. The rest of the MPs will choose the leader of the opposition. The leader of the opposition will choose the shadow cabinet.

10. A leader of MPs will be chosen for a state or a group of states where the number of MPs is less than 20.

11. If the PM resigns within five years of the term, the 2nd in the PM election will be chosen as the next PM.

12. For the Rajya Sabha, the members should never contest in any general election of MLA or MP.

13. Rajya Sabha members should choose between the parliamentary salary or their own income.

14. Only cabinet ministers should be allowed to have a diplomatic passport as long as they remain in office.

# A FEW RANDOM THOUGHTS

Sometimes I get random thoughts! Some of them are relevant, and some of them are irrelevant. Here I place them together.

## CIVILIZATION

We are all familiar with the word "Civilization". But what do we understand by it? Does civilization mean obeying a set of rules or covering ourselves with proper clothes? Looking at history, we find that civilization started with a group of people trying to protect themselves and their belongings, which were mostly cattle herds in the beginning. Afterwards, humans started cultivation and worked on improving their daily tools. Then came individual property rights regarding land, cattle, food etc.

From the individual property rights, there came another important concept, which was theft. No one should take another person's belongings without their consent. However, human life is limited. Who is going to possess someone's property after their death? Here comes the idea of inheritance and family. This gave rise to the most frightening thought for an individual. What if someone does not have any inheritance? Human beings realized how feeble they were against the rules of nature. Even now, we do not know what is waiting for us at the very next moment. Thus started a human's fight with their inner weaknesses, which led to the idea of something unchangeable or absolute, beyond the transient world of our experience. Finally, humans became civilized!

## DHARMA AND RELIGION

In the whole Indian subcontinent, Dharma is an important subject. It is commonly used as a direct translation of the word religion. However, if we try to understand Dharma, it is better translated as the word ethics or moral values. On the other hand, religion is a more organized system, more often backed up by a political State. Most religions have hard and fast belief in the creator of the universe/world and follow the teachings of some particular books. In comparison, Dharma and religion are not the same, and Dharma plays a much more important role in society!

Let us try to understand the relationship between Dharma and religion. When a particular social/economic value system gets recognized by a State, then it becomes a religion. Example;

1. Emperor Ashoka formed a political State on the teaching of Gautama Buddha.
2. The Soviet socialist republic was formed on the idea of Class struggle written by Karl Marks.
3. Pakistan and Israel are two political States based on two religions.

Dharma is the most fundamental concept in the Indian way of life. Then comes the Artha, Kama and Moksha (described as Nirvana in Buddhism). In easy words, whatever is good for society as a whole (beyond individuals) is called Dharma. We can also say that the collection of **Justice, Honesty, Dedication and Compassion, Mercifulness, and Renunciation** is called Dharma. However, it is very difficult to find all those qualities together. The developed world is built upon the foundation of the former three. In contrast, the developing countries stress more on the latter three. To meet at the middle ground, we could consider our lives as composed of three phases.

1. A student (financially dependent on their parents).
2. Individuals with earning capacities.
3. A retired person.

In the first stage of life, one should cultivate the first three qualities: **Justice, Honesty, and Dedication.** As one starts earning, one should be careful of being **Compassionate**

**along with the first three qualities.** At the last stage of life, one should concentrate on **Mercifulness and Renunciation.** On the other hand, those who choose the monastic life should concentrate on **Renunciation only.**

# KARMA (ACTION) AND KARMAFAL (REACTION)

The word karma (action) is already popular in the West. Also popular in the entire Indian subcontinent, karma is a link between the philosophy of dharma and the followers of ritualistic religion. This brings together the people who believe in multiple births and those who do not.

Now, let us think about the concept of karmafal (the fruits/consequences of karma). In general, if Person A harms Person B in some way, the first one (Person A) will get some punishment in future. If we accept this idea, how do we know that Person B did not do something wrong in the past, and this was their punishment? So, person A should not be punished, and we could never know who committed the first crime!

Let us try to understand Karma and Karmafal in a different way. If someone does some good work, that itself is their karmafal of the past. Similarly, if someone does something wrong, that is their karmafal of the past. That means if someone does a crime today, they are going to do another crime in future unless it goes through a punishment system. The punishment is to save the individual from their own karmafal. On the other hand, someone having poverty or misfortune should never be blamed on their karmafal. Some people are honest, even if poor; that should be considered as the good karmafal of their past. On the other hand, some people are dishonest, even if rich, that should be considered as the bad karma of their past.

# EDUCATION

We must have no doubt that Justice is the most important thing for a society to flourish. And we can introduce justice into our society only through education. What is education? It is a system that builds in an individual the ability for original thinking and a sense of responsibility, which means being aware of the consequences of one's actions. An educated person is expected to communicate with their family and social surroundings with some basic decency. This is the basic expectation of education. In the whole Indian subcontinent, presently, there are two education systems (public and private systems). From the school level to the university, the examinations are extremely difficult to crack. From a student's point of view, exam systems function like black boxes. The higher education system is plagued by too much politics and reservations. As a result, very few students attempt a PhD, which has its own inherent complications. Let us try to think about how to improve the education system in India. Here are my proposals,

Primary and Secondary Education:

1. Until the 10$^{th}$ STD, i.e. for students of age approximately less than 16 years, there should not be any boarding school.
2. Until the 6$^{th}$ STD, education should be focused on mathematics, language, grammar, and spelling.
3. For secondary education, work education and physical education should be compulsory.
4. There should be some senior-junior mixed classes promoting interaction.
5. Students studying in Indian languages should study an additional subject in English. Those who study in English should take an additional subject in some Indian language.
6. Each school should be run by a managing committee from the retired teachers and staff of that school elected by the existing

staff members and teachers. Each committee should be validated for three years. The committee members will not be reappointed.

7. School teachers should not take any money for private tuition. The alumni Association of a school should pay some money to the teachers as an encouragement for the additional service.

8. The school committee should keep in contact with the ex-students weekly at first, then monthly/ yearly manner.

9. Each school should open a section for elderly people aged more than 60 years with the provision for mid-day meals with/without payment.

10. No one should be allowed a caste-based reservation until they study in a government-aided public secondary school.

Higher Secondary Education:

1. More and more schools should be organized as boarding schools.

2. Students should be encouraged to learn an additional Indian language other than Hindi, English or their own vernacular.

3. No one should be allowed a caste-based reservation until they study in a government-aided public secondary school.

4. Basic political science and computer awareness should be compulsory for higher secondary education.

Examination system:

For the primary education system, there should be a yearly individual assessment without any pass/fail. For the secondary system, the final year assessment of promotion or not should be divided into four parts.

1. Closed book exam: Marked by the teachers (students should get back the examination paper after marking) (30%).

2. A compulsory home assignment of the same closed-book examination with all compulsory questions. This will be marked by a senior student at the same school, supervised by the teacher (students should get back the exam paper after marking). (30%)
3. Marking of a junior student's assignment at the same school, supervised by the teacher. (30%)
4. Individual assessment of students by the class teacher. (10%)

## College system

1. Youth hostels should be available for more and more students in the city.
2. Students should be encouraged to learn a foreign language like Arabic, Persian, Chinese, Japanese, Spanish, German, French etc.
3. Basic economics, accounting, and environmental science should be compulsory for college education.
4. All the exams should be transparent, i.e., students should get back the exam paper after marking.
5. Each college should be run by a governing body chosen from the retired teachers/staff by the existing teacher, staff and students for three years. No one should be elected for more than one term.
6. No political student union should be allowed on campus.
7. No one should be allowed a caste-based reservation until they study in a government-aided public college.

## University education

1. Everyone should be supposed to write a thesis for the University Graduation.

2. Philosophy and ethics should be compulsory subjects for University Graduates.
3. The University should be run by a governing body chosen from the retired teachers/staff by the existing teacher, staff, and students for three years. No one should be elected for more than one term.
4. No one should be allowed a caste-based reservation until they study in a gov.-aided public university.
5. No political student union should be allowed on campus.
6. All the exams should be transparent, i.e., students should get back the exam paper after marking.
7. For any recruitment (teachers/staff), there should be a transparent list (in terms of marking) of the candidates who have applied for that job. The list should be sent to all the candidates who applied for the job.

PhD and Research

1. Universities and research institutes should have a managing committee elected by the existing teachers, students and staff and the retired professor for three years. No one should be elected for more than one term.
2. Every PhD candidate must publish one/two first-author articles in peer review journal to get the PhD degree; otherwise, if they write only a thesis, then they should be awarded an MPhil degree.
3. The managing committee should interview each PhD student after 2/3 years about the graduation of their PhD.
4. The PhD Graduates should be encouraged to start spin-out companies as well as non-governmental charitable organizations.

# WORK-LIFE

After the completion of education, one is expected to start working and earning. Students sometimes take a temporary break to prepare for government jobs. These jobs are difficult to crack but prestigious in the end. In my opinion, the central government of India-Bharat should not recruit any employees directly. After serving state governments for ten years, an employee should be eligible for a central government job. For state government jobs, those who are still a student should be given more preference. For any job, there are four parts.

1. The work to be done and the salary/earning in return. (30%)
2. The supervisor (Not for businesspeople) (30%)
3. The coworkers/employees (30%)
4. The transportation between home and work. (10%)

Among those four, at least 50% should be favourable for anyone to continue the job. There are some common rules for any paid job.

1. We should try to keep a record of each day's work time and the duties performed.
2. Try to build up savings for six months as soon as possible.
3. Never consider the breach of confidentiality or blackmail the employer.

Compared to other jobs, agricultural jobs are very different in present Bharat. In most states, agriculture is not as profitable as a full-time job. To solve that problem, we should redefine our farmers; anyone receiving a government salary or pension should not be allowed to own agricultural land anymore.

# MARRIAGE

Marriage forms an important part of most people's lives. All of us should search for suitable life partners. In India, traditional arranged marriages have existed for a long time. At present, both arranged marriages and self-arranged or so-called love marriages are prevalent. Both systems have their own merits. However, an individual must decide which one is good for them.

Those who want to marry by themselves must need to be financially independent and at least 22 years old. If the monthly income of the partners is equivalent, then it is even better. They should have known each other for a sufficiently long period of time, usually for more than about three years. In this kind of marriage, caste, religion etc., are not important. But, for peaceful cohabitation, the partners should be considerate of each other's food habits. No social ritual is mandatory, but a joint bank account with equal status for the partners is required. Before marriage, the partners should have a clear discussion about their future living arrangements, which should decide the address in their joint account.

Those who are getting married through family arrangements should consider the decision of their parents to be more important in this regard. In that case, a common friend between the two families can prove to be more helpful. An equivalent family background will be beneficial for the success of the marriage. For arranged marriages, one needs some social rituals. Initially, the two families should visit each other's houses in the presence of their relatives. It is more helpful if the relatives are from different economic backgrounds. The most important point of discussion should be the future living arrangements for the married couple (House/ room/toilets). The wife may come to live in the husband's family house or vice versa. A clear discussion of this must be done prior to the marriage. A joint bank account with the decided address should be opened within 30 days of the marriage ceremony.

For any marriage, the age should be more than 22 years for both bride and groom. In a marriage ceremony, the eligible (age + finance) bachelors and spinsters should be introduced to each other from both sides.

# FAMILY

A family is the structural unit of a civilized society anywhere in the world. In the developed world, a family usually consists of parents and kids. As the kids grow up and start earning, they are expected to start their own families. College/ University students sometimes spend time with their grandparents. On the other hand, in the developing world, a family includes more people and has a much more complicated structure in terms of finances and other responsibilities. Sometimes more financial responsibilities are enforced on some individuals, which is certainly wrong.

For a family of parents and kids, the responsibility of the parents universally is to earn enough for a month and to spend responsibly. If we consider the other responsibilities of a family, then list them as follows.

1.  Shopping Regular.
2.  Shopping Occasional.
3.  Laundry.
4.  Cleaning of toilets.
5.  Cooking regular.
6.  Cooking occasional
7.  Dishwashing.
8.  House repair
9.  Garbage cleaning etc.

The couple should help each other with household chores like laundry, cleaning, shopping etc. and other daily requirements of a family. However, the most important responsibility of a family is to raise the kids with justice and a sense of equality. For a family with multiple kids, the parents should never consider one of them to be more important than the others. It is even worse if the parents expect some children to consider themselves to be secondary to their siblings.

# RETIREMENTS

Every person working up to 55/65 years of age deserves a retirement. However, for the majority of people in India, there is no substantial pension. The State should offer pensions to every working individual, according to the direct taxes paid during their working years. The retirement age for Group D staff should not be more than 55 years.

# AFTER DEATH

Death is the ultimate reality for all living beings. Are we afraid of dying? Yes, but we are more afraid of losing our loved ones. Probably, even more, distressing is the question, what will be our responsibilities at the time we lose someone we love? Death comes in many forms.

1. Premature death before marriage or before having any inheritance. This is the most difficult time for a parent. We do not need any funeral service or social ritual for this. We need to find some friends of the deceased person to take care of the grief-stricken parents. We can plant trees in the memory of that leaving soul.

2. A person can have a premature death after getting married and having kids. We do not need any social rituals such as a funeral service. Rather, we need a responsible person (probably a local retired schoolteacher, one who is not a relative) who can keep an eye on all the dependents for some time. The main purpose of this is to ensure that everyone gets a fair share of the inheritance.

3. If a person dies in old age after having grandsons/granddaughters, there is no need for sadness. We should perform all the social

rituals. The cost should be divided among all the successors. The heirs should say a few words in memory of the deceased person. It is worth keeping them on record.

# PHILOSOPHY/DARSHAN

In Indian civilization, philosophy was considered to be the highest knowledge, above even science and technology. At the same time, history and documentation were supposed to be the least important things. Now, what do we understand about philosophy/Darshan? Since ancient times, Indian philosophers have been trying to address questions like, what is the cause behind the Universe? Why did it happen? This has given rise to vast knowledge systems. The primary of all those philosophies is the Sankhya Darshan. The main idea is that the universe is composed of changeable (Prakriti) and unchangeable (Purusha). At the later stage, the Vedanta darshan says the primal cause of this universe is that unchangeable, the absolute, and we are that absolute (Brahman).

# AVATAR

In Indian philosophy, the creator Brahma is not given much importance. On the contrary, Rama and Krishna, the heroes of the two Indian epics, the Ramayana and the Mahabharata, are considered to be the Avatars of Lord Vishnu. The idea is that all human beings are the manifestations of the primal cause, Brahman. But we see more of that manifestation in some human beings than others. These rare human beings are termed Avatars. The good thing about this is that there can be more Avatars coming in the future. Are you curious if you are an Avatar or not? Take this simple test.

1. Clean all the plastics around us.
2. Stop the sound pollution in India.

3. Stop the air pollution in India.
4. Clean the rivers in India.
5. Find a home for all the street dogs in India.

Within 100 years, people will call you an Avatar! Are we ready to be the next Avatar?

# HOW DID I WRITE THE BOOK?

## Taipei, Taiwan

On September 20th 2009, I started my journey to Taiwan for a PhD in Biophotonics at the National Yang-Ming University. The previous months proved to be very stressful as I collected all the necessary documents for the upcoming travel. One of the most difficult tasks was collecting the Passport urgently (via the Tatkal service). I remember spending one night on the Brabourne Road footpath in Kolkata for the passport application. The second tricky task was to collect 2000 USD to show that I had enough money to sustain myself for the first few days in Taiwan. It is important to mention that the rule of 2000 USD was not officially written anywhere. It was made aware by the TECC, Delhi, only verbally. The pre-requisition to get USD in India was to have a visa (as told to me by the State Bank of India). But according to the TECC, I needed the USD first. So, it was like an egg-chicken problem. Which one was to be solved first? Finally, I got 2000 USD on 09/09/09, the date is still written on my passport, and it changed my life.

I arrived at Taipei Taoyuan International Airport on 21/09/2009, then took a bus to Taipei's main station by myself. My would-be PhD supervisor was waiting for me at the bus station. We took a taxi to Yang-Ming University. In the evening, my supervisor took me to the nearest Carrefour supermarket for shopping and then dropped me back at the student dormitory. This warm gesture helped me absorb the first shock in a new place.

This was the first time I had been so far away from my hometown Kolkata. I could not speak good English, only a few words in Mandarin/Chinese. However, I could still manage my life in Taipei because of the Taipei metro, perhaps the best metro in the world! I could not but share one of my memories of the Taipei metro. One day, I saw a person with some visual problem being assisted by the metro staff to ride the train. I was really worried about how the gentleman was going to get down to his destination station. To my surprise, another metro staff came into the train after a few stops and helped him get down the train. I realized that there must have been some telephone connection between the metro staff. It was something new for me!

I spent the first year in Taiwan without a phone number. During my first two years in Taiwan, I stayed in the student dormitory sharing with two of my friends. One of them was from Assam and another from Assam, but with Bengali mother tongue. In the 2nd year, four other friends came to the same dormitory, one of them from Himachal Pradesh, one from west-Bengal, one from Assam with Bengali mother tongue and one from Tamilnadu. In 2010 and 2011, there were only a few Indians in Taiwan. I often went to National Taiwan University for my experiments, as I did not have the required instruments at NYMU. During the weekends, our friends were mostly together, going up to the University playground, chatting among ourselves and cooking together. Within the first year, I could speak fluent Assamese and understood ALPHA, SALPHA etc. I knew about Sankardev and Kumarilla Bhatta. In the 2nd year, when one of our friends from Himachal Pradesh joined, we started discussing more and more Indian philosophy. The Assamese friend was a non-believer in any creator. The friend from Himachal was a believer in the creator of this universe. I could agree with them both to some extent. But personally, I had some preference for the Advaita philosophy of Shankaracharya. We discussed intensely over hours in Hindi as well as in English. At some point, we could realize that none of those languages was sufficient and regretted our ignorance of the Sanskrit language. We promised each other that one day we would try to learn Sanskrit. In Taiwan, one of the best things that happened to me was that I received a reply email from Dr A. P. J. Abdul Kalam. I realized the power of the internet!

Towards the end of my second year in Taiwan, I bought my first personal laptop (2011). I started working with a new PhD supervisor and moved to Academia Sinica, although I was still a student at NYMU. I did not have to do the PhD coursework again for this. I just needed to do sufficient research to write my PhD thesis. Academia Sinica was the best research institution in Taiwan. So, most of the international students came there through the TIGP program. However, I was still a student with an NYMU fellowship for the year 2011 (July) to 2012 (July). My life became very isolated at NanKang (Academia Sinica) compared to Shipai (NYMU). The weather at Nankang was even worse. It rained a lot. The weekends were extremely lonely. The only friend I had then was the internet. This was the time when I watched the full series of Story of India by Michel Woods. I was mesmerized by the narration of Mr Woods. I can not forget the part where he described the last few words from Buddha "All the created things must pass, strive on diligently."

Onwards the summer of 2012, I made some new friends who came through the TIGP program; they were from Pakistan. To be honest, they were/are really nice! We could have open-minded discussions on history, religion and philosophy. I could learn many things about the partition of India, especially about Junagarh, Hyderabad and Kashmir. I was surprised to learn why UN Resolution 1949 was fulfilled in Kashmir. At that time, it was unknown to most of the Bharatiya. Thanks to Mr Tareq Fatah, now many people know about it.

In early 2013, I took four of my Taiwanese friends to India. We went to Delhi, stayed one day there, then to Agra and Benaras, and finally Benaras to Kolkata. My elder brother helped me organize the trip. All through the trip, people thought of me as a local resident working as a travel guide. I realized that nobody could distinguish me from one province of India to another. By September 2013, another student came to TIGP. He was from my home state of West Bengal. I did not know him before. But he became one of the best friends of my life. We realized that the bond created by a common language is much stronger than anything else. By the end of 2013, one significant thing happened. I got a secondhand iPhone 4 for 4000 National Taiwanese Dollars. It changed my life completely. It's hard to believe now that I could live without a smartphone a few years ago. (Sadly, I lost the phone in 2016 in my hometown Kolkata.)

In April 2014, I went to Sydney, Australia, to present my research work at a scientific conference. I got to know two Indians from Kerala who helped me find a place for a few days. They also introduced me to delicious vegetarian food in Sydney. I met a PhD student from Bangladesh at the conference. He also took me to a nice restaurant. All three of them were nice, and I had a great time with all three of them. Let me mention two other incidents that happened in Australia. One day during the conference lunch, I took a break looking for a train ride to cross the Sydney Harbour Bridge and come back. At the station, I met a brilliant Australian Gentleman and had a chat about India, cricket, Sydney etc. Eventually, I came to know that his car was broken, and he was going to pick up an alternate car for a few days. Incidentally, he was going in the same direction as me. Then he asked me about my plan. I told him that my plan was to get down after the bridge and take another train to come back to the conference. Hearing that, he offered me a car ride close to my conference. I was delighted!

After my conference, I kept one day visiting the city. In the morning, I was waiting at the train station. One gentleman in a traditional Arabic dress came to me and greeted me in Arabic. I also greeted him back in Arabic. He was very happy and asked me if I was from Pakistan. I replied that I was from India. We introduced ourselves. Learning that he was from Bangladesh, we started to talk in Bengali. On the train, we chatted a bit more. I learned that he was doing some research on cancer. It turned out that both of us were using the cancer drug cisplatin in our research. Very surprising!

2014, I went to another conference in the USA, San Antonio. Initially, my visa was rejected. But then I reapplied for the visa with letters from my PhD supervisors. This time I got the visa. It was a long flight from Taipei to San Francisco, then another flight to San Antonio. I started on Saturday and also reached on Saturday. In the evening, I collected my dinner at the gas station. It was Mexican food, but I confused it to be Indian food at first. The next day, I went to visit the conference venue and met a Bangladeshi student from South Korea. We had many discussions about childhood readings, politics, history etc. From the conference in San Antonio, I got a postdoc offer. By November 2014, I had submitted my PhD thesis. It was time to pack up. My next destination was Montreal, Canada.

If I did not go to Taiwan, I might still have done PhD somewhere else. However, I could never learn what I learnt in Taiwan, the best place in the world! If I could tell you my thoughts about Taiwan and mainland China's relationship, they would be,

1. Taiwan, Hong Kong, Macau and PRC should join the Olympics together.
2. Taiwan, Hong Kong, and Macau should be allowed to join the United Nations.
3. In the third stage, PRC should consider all its citizens as a member of the communist party and include them in voting.
4. At the final stage, Tibet and Xinjiang should be allowed to join the United Nations.

I really hope to see these things happening in the near future!

## Montreal, Quebec, Canada

In the early March of 2015, I started my journey to Canada from Kolkata. My first stop was Chennai, southern India. The next flight was to the next morning to London after an overnight wait. The flight to London took an emergency landing in Bucharest, Romania, due to a medical emergency. I reached London Heathrow several hours behind the scheduled time. After a few hours of waiting, I could board the final flight to Montreal. I was really exhausted at the end of my journey. The good thing came in the end, my post-doc host came to receive me at the Montreal airport and lent me some warm clothes.

It was my first encounter with snow. The very next day was -30 degrees C. I went to apply for my social insurance number. It was an easy process, but the address of the office was given wrong, which made me wonder for more than an hour in the snow. I could open a bank account very easily. However, getting a phone sim was not very easy. It was very expensive too.

After a few months, I could realize that Canada is a coexistence between two States, Quebec and the rest of Canada. Somehow, it works perfectly fine! I was affiliated with Polytechnique Montreal (UdM), but I worked mostly at CrCHUM downtown. So, I commuted between the two places regularly. Once the winter was over, it was a really nice time with long daylight for sixteen-seventeen hours. However, I still regret that I did not visit Niagara even once within the two years, despite living so close to it.

By the end of September 2015, a sad incident happened in Uttar Pradesh, India, that really shocked me. Within a few days, I tried to organize my thoughts and wrote a piece on social media, "Save the cow, but no ban on beef."

*Recently India witnessed a really sad incident in Dadri for which no criticism seems enough. Any politics with this incident is least expected. However, the communal politics in the name of beef ban or beef party goes on. In India, a large number of people are vegetarian. Among the non-vegetarian, there are two classes, those who eat beef and those who cannot. The first class of people argues that if someone can eat goat or lamb then why not beef, as long as it is cheaper than the other meats. They also argue that a plant also has life, so it does not mean that a vegetarian is not killing anything. It is even more sinful to kill a plant. We may try to think the answer in this way. All the animals depend on the plant directly or indirectly for food. However, a vegetarian eats mostly the grains (paddy, wheat etc) or the stored food of a plant (potato), when the plant is already dead or the fruits (for those tree lives more than one year). Consuming green vegetables do not serve the appetite but some people eat that for cellulose or vitamins. However, being a vegetarian is a really difficult task. One needs to eat a lot of food. Now, if we try to think the reason why some people do not eat beef then we land on an answer which is purely economic and not religious at all. There are three things; cow, bull and ox. I do not think anyone is going eat a cow as long as it gives milk. There are only a few bulls (these are required for reproduction). Only remaining is the ox (which was required for cultivation and physical labor). In India, more than 70% people were farmers (even in China, those who were farmer does not eat beef still today). For them, an ox was always the most valuable property. But this was a movable property which is really difficult to protect from theft. And if people eat beef then it is really easy to hide the theft. So, there might be some ruler who realized that and made some law not to eat beef. And with time it became a religious belief. However, with the passage of time the situation has changed a lot. With the modern technology, animal power is replaced by machines. Now days a man does not depend on animals for physical labor. Then what will happen to those oxen and old cows (which stopped giving milk)? Is the slaughterhouse the only destination for them? The Government can play a significant role to solve this question. They can build shelters for those cows and oxen in the most under developed places of the country. Bio-gas, as a source of energy, natural fertilizer and pesticides can be produced there (even the Government can pay subsidy to those centers). Collections of vegetable waste can be organized which in turn will make the cities cleaner. At the end when the animal gets its natural death several products can be obtained from it. In this way the poor people can get employment and the country can build its self-sustained energy sources. Finally, hope we can live in a place where we try to understand each other's views and agree to disagree.*

After several years, when I think about that incident, I get two sets of thoughts.

1. We do not know what actually happened on that day.
2. It is really brave that a young man could say before all the TV channels, "Majhab nehi sikhata apas mein byar rakhna," within just a few days of his father's death.

During the winter of 2015-16, I read a few books:

1. India wins freedom, by Maulana Abul Kalam Azad
2. Transfer of Power in India, by V. P. Menon
3. Pakistan or the Partition, by Dr B. R. Ambedkar
4. Development of Metaphysics in Persia, by Md. Iqbal

Initially, I wanted to write a series on the partition and independence of India. But I could not manage it because of time. In India, there are two big unsolved issues at present.

1. The religious conflict between two major groups.
2. Caste system and reservations.

I wanted to understand the caste system in detail. I read the book written by Dr Ambedkar, 'Annihilation of caste', 'Revolution-and-counter revolution in India' (partly), and 'Buddha and His Dhamma'. I realized that on many occasions, we misunderstand the caste system (Jati Vyavastha) and Social Class system (Varna Vyavastha). In the social class system, there were four groups: Brahmins, Kshatriya, Vaisya, and Shudra. Those four groups indicated intellectuals, Statesmen, businesspersons, and workers. There was another word that Sraman that needs attention. Initially, my understanding was that Varna Vyavastha probably started with the four groups Brahmin, Sraman, Kshatriya and Vaishya. Then the Buddhist monks took the name Sraman whereas workers were assigned another name, Shudra. I wrote an article about it, "A manifesto towards caste-free society India", and sent it to the NYT (2016). No wonder they did not publish my article. I sent my article to many people, one of them being a very prominent historian in India. She replied to my email, although she did not agree with my idea. I was nevertheless greatly delighted to receive a reply email from her. Then I read a book written by her, which certainly improved my understanding of Indian history.

In 2016, I went to a scientific conference in Dublin, Ireland, to present our scientific research. At that conference, I met one Indian PhD student from Taiwan. We became very good friends. On the way back, I missed my flight from Heathrow to Montreal. So, I was allowed to enter the UK for one night and stayed in a hotel organized by the airline. The next morning, I came back to the airport and took the tube to London. I could never imagine how crowded it could be! Somehow, I managed to go up to the Tower of London, took some pictures of the posters of the crown (I did not enter the tower) and came back to the airport.

Towards the end of 2016, India witnessed a major economic crisis. Five-hundred- and one-thousand-rupee bank notes were removed from circulation overnight by the central government led by Prime Minister Narendra Modi. Initially, everyone thought it to be a great strategy to remove illegal money (not taxed properly) as well as fake currency. However, after a few months, almost all the demonetized money came back to the RBI, though many people still have some of those demonetized notes. I personally had a few thousand. In my opinion, demonetization taught us a big lesson; that is, developing countries have approximately 30-50 % of grey economics based on currency notes. However, that grey economics is fed into the good economy connected to the taxation system. If we want to remove the grey economy overnight, that is going to affect the good economics too.

By the end of January 2017, I had left Canada. My next destination was the UK for another post-doc position.

## SOUTHAMPTON, ENGLAND, THE UK

I came to the UK in June 2017. It took me a few months to get the visa as I was rejected once for not submitting the NARIC English language certificate. I am still thankful that my employers gave me another certificate of sponsorship. After arriving in the UK, I could get a phone SIM at the central bus stop at Heathrow. However, I suffered a lot in opening a bank account. Once it was done, my daily life was much easier than anywhere else before! Starting at the University, I found that everything had a proper training method, e.g. the purchasing for the laboratory. I should specially mention a course on Equality and Diversity that I had to take, which was compulsory for every newcomer. It told me a very nice thing, every one of us is a minority in some aspects and a majority in some other aspects. For example, if I consider myself an Indian in the UK working at the University of Southampton, I am a minority. But If I consider myself to be a man, then I belong to the majority within the research group. The course was indeed helpful in starting a new postdoc life.

The first thing that surprised me in the UK was so many secondhand stores run by various charitable organizations. In those stores, I could buy many things at minimum prices. If India had similar secondhand stores, my life would have been much better in my childhood.

I came back to India during the 2017 Christmas break. Two significant things happened during that trip.

1. I attended the Indian History Congress 2017 at Jadavpur University, Kolkata.
2. I could not complete the standalone KYC for mutual funds investment in India.

For the Indian History Congress, I presented my article about the caste system to the Ancient India section. The conference was very poorly managed. However, I could see historians like Professor Habib speaking to everyone without any security or police protection. It was my bad luck that Professor Thapar did not attend the first day of the conference. On the second day, I went very late to the conference, as I had to go to Park Street for the stand-alone KYC for mutual funds. In my previous visit to the mutual fund office in Salt Lake, Kolkata, I was not allowed to do stand-alone KYC, which means KYC without any policy of mutual fund investment. This time I went to an office at Park Street and had some heated argument about why I could not have the stand-alone KYC done. The Officer-in-charge could not show me any rule forbidding it. Finally, he told me to find a document that says stand-alone KYC is allowed. A typical example of a negative argument! However, I came back and made some written complaints about them. But I never heard back from them. This is called Indian bureaucracy! Once I came to the UK, I wrote some emails to the Indian History Congress regarding the arrangements for the conference. However, the conference became very irregular onwards.

In 2018, I attended two scientific conferences, one in Nantes, France, and another one in Kausiang, Taiwan. However, I would like to mention another special event that happened at the University of Southampton. The Chief Justice of India (Supreme Court), Mr Deepak Misra, came to the University after one of the milestone verdicts about LGBTQ rights in India. In his talk, Mr Misra explained how this verdict was going to change Indian society. There was a question-answer session after the talk. I also wanted to ask some questions about the Indian Constitution to him but could not manage the courage. Albeit, it was a great experience to see him face-to-face.

By the end of 2018, I really wanted to save Air India, so I wrote a pamphlet.

*A Plan to Revive Air-India:*

*We all know that currently, Air India (AI) is going through a tough time. Although there are reports that the government is planning to sell it, no customer has been found yet. Here, we would like to find the problems and propose some solutions to revive AI.*

*Problems:*

*1. All over the world, the aviation industry got a setback due to the high fuel price and competition among the airlines.*

*2. AI, like other government institutions, is not free from political influence. It suffers from a load of a huge number of employees, some of whom might get employed under pressure from politicians but do not have the required skills.*

*3. Lack of effective plans for further development.*

*Solutions:*

*1. The solution for global economics is beyond our scope. We could try to find the solutions for the rest of the problems.*

*2. The employees could be divided into several groups. Considering the present situation, the executives should take a 30% salary cut, pilots and cabin crews should take a 20% salary cut, and technical ground staff should take a 10% salary cut.*

*3. The office staffs should be allowed to form entrepreneur franchisees to operate under contract with AI. Otherwise, they should be offered voluntary retirement from the service.*

*4. The head office and the aero-plane hub of Air-India should be transferred to Kolkata, which should have a lower maintenance cost for office and aircraft.*

*5. Each passenger should be given a language option during the booking and the cabin crew should use the language opted for by the majority of the passengers. However, even the single linguistic minority passenger should be addressed with the written document. (for example, safety demonstration)*

*6. There is not a single connection from Kolkata or Dhaka to Europe. Two new routes; Dhaka, Kolkata- Frankfurt and Dhaka, Kolkata- Heathrow would catch the eyes of the passengers with their preferred languages.*

*7. There should be some collaboration with railways to exchange passengers. For example, AI can arrange tickets and transportation towards the next journey by Indian railways on payment.*

*8. Finally, my personal experience with Air-India is very good and I wish the government should stop any idea of liquidation of that company.*

In February 2019, I wrote an imaginary story about public transport in India/Kolkata on Facebook.

*Board exam 2019 English suggestion; Safe drive, save life:*

*Kolkata, January 2019: Dear students, we are very close to our Board exam 2019, for English a very important topic would be writing an essay on "safe drive, save life." So, do we plan to prepare it now? Said the teacher.*

*Ayan, a very bright student, replied, Sir! It might be a good idea to search on the Internet about this topic before starting to write.*

*True! In that case, we will be completely aware of the government instructions, added Gita. So, lets search on our phone. Hurry!*

*Yes, we got some, it says that safe drive, save live is an awareness program initiated by the chief minister of West Bengal in 2016. It became very popular and reduced the number of road accidents. Kolkata traffic police and Kolkata police jointly organize the campaign. Said Ayan.*

*How about the civic police? They also take part in this campaign, right? Asked Gita.*

*Surely, I believe they play a major role in traffic control nowadays. Replied Anita.*

*So we got some information about this campaign. It is a very popular one also effective. Do we have some ideas to improve this campaign? Any idea guys? The teacher paused a bit.*

*Soumya, sitting in the corner, looked around at everyone and then with immense politeness started, it is a nice campaign. However, we still have plenty of problems. Still many of us are unaware to wear the helmet during biking. Reckless driving of busses is still there. Our infrastructure is not enough to manage pedestrian and motor vehicles at the same time. Moreover, problems with the taxi, I have completely forgotten when did I ride a taxi on meter last time!*

*I agree that the problem of the taxi in Kolkata is a serious one, but not sure whether we can discuss it under the safe drive, save life context. Said the teacher.*

*Soumya replied, I went to the Airport yesterday early morning to drop my elder sister, who was flying to New Delhi. We went to the Airport in a rental car. I wanted to wait at the airport until my sister is done with the security checking. Then I wanted to find a cab to return my home. However, the taxi driver rejected to go on the meter. I asked him should I call the police. He became even angrier and tried to call his fellow drivers. I promptly took a picture of the car and stepped back. Finally, I got an appraisal from him that my father must be a very rich man. I went down to lodge a complaint. However, there was no one in the police booth. So, I took another picture. I could have been to the CISF, though it is my personal experience they sometimes say that they do not understand Bengali. Then I caught a bus to the airport gate no 2, crossed the Jessore road without any traffic, stopped another bus without a stoppage and came to my home.*

*You got a fairly bad experience. Said the teacher, though you managed the situation smartly. However, please do not have personal bitterness against that particular person. He might be a good person, got overnight work or distressed with personal problems. And I believe the real problem lies elsewhere. The distance of the Jessore road from the airport terminal is more than 2 km, and each driver gets a long waiting time to enter the airport. We need a bus and taxi stand at Jessore road and a shuttle bus should ferry between Jessore road and the airport terminal. We should try to find the solutions by ourselves. Sometimes we pedestrians do not follow the traffic rule and do not walk along the left side of the road as well. Stopped the teacher.*

*After some silence, Jaya said "Sir! I do have a question."*

*Yes, please go ahead. Replied the teacher.*

*Is it rational for pedestrians to walk along the left side of the road? How about the pedestrians use the right edge of the road and the motor vehicles use the conventional left side of the road. In that case, pedestrian and the motor driver can see them face to face and the pedestrians can position themselves accordingly. This will reduce sound pollution due to air horns reasonably.*

*This idea surprised everyone. Finally, the teacher broke up the silence. Hmm! We should think a bit more before implementing this kind of idea. We should also consider the competition between busses and auto-rickshaws.*

*Sir, do you think this is a good idea to operate buses and auto-rickshaws on the same route? Asked Gita.*

*I would rather prefer separate routes for bus and auto-rickshaws. Replied Ayan, there should not be any bus route without road divider within the city, even heavy vehicles more than 3 tons should not be allowed inside the city without a road divider. And there should not be any auto-rickshaw shuttle within a bus route. At any time there should not be more than two lanes of motor vehicles from the road divider and no overtake from the left side. There should be camera surveillance in some critical points, drivers violating the traffic rules will be sent to the driving test again.*

*I would also suggest that spot fine by the police surgeons should be stopped completely. If anyone breaks the rule repeatedly then he/she must be tried before the judge. Good and experienced drivers should be graded for higher payments for commercial vehicles. Said Soumya.*

*So we got a nice discussion on this topic. Please take it as a home task to write it as an article. Just to mention it should be "a safe drive saves the life" or "safe drive, saves the life." Thank you, guys! Concluded the teacher.*

*PS: This conversation is completely imaginary, however, there are some pictures and bus tickets taken on December 6th, 2018.*

In 2018 and 2019, I went outside the UK several times. It was really difficult to enter back to the UK through Heathrow as it took a long time to cross the border with non-European passports. I am still very surprised that I am not allowed to use the smart gate even though I have the BRP from the UK as well as I am a legal taxpayer in the UK. However, I would like to mention that I never had any bad experiences during border crossing. Every time the staff there were really nice to me.

In 2019, Mr Javed Akhtar and Mrs Shabana Azmi came to the University of Southampton. It was a really nice experience to attend their talk. After the talk, I went to Mr Akhtar and had a few words. My last scientific conference was in Basel, Switzerland, in 2019. After the conference, I went to a place I had never heard about before, a small place called Thollon-les-Memises (France), close to the city of Avian on the bank of Geneva Lake. That is the best place I have ever been in my life.

Onward 2019, I wanted to write my ideas on social networking media. It really began during the COVID lockdown. I wrote a series about the partition and independence of India in Bengali in August 2020. By the end of 2021, I was planning to apply for Indefinite Leave to Remain in the UK. I prepared for the Life in the UK test. It taught me many things about the State of the UK. I felt that the test should be compulsory for anyone participating in the UK elections as well as all the new voters.

After several years in the UK, I must say I like the country as well as the State. I have joined the local street cleaning group to make our locality better. If I ever get any opportunity to make the country better, I wouldn't think twice. I have a personal dream to have a direct flight between London Heathrow and Kolkata airports (even once a week).

# POSTFACE
# WE, AS INDIVIDUALS!

Since the dawn of civilization, the Indian mind has been trying to find the answer to the question, Who am I? Am I something beyond the body and mind? Who is considered to be successful in this world? To answer these questions, we have to start from the material world. Suppose I am an individual between 22-65 years of age, married, and earning person. The life of such a person is like a light bulb. Primarily, we are connected to our power source, which is our professional life. As a married individual, the personal life consists of the relationship with the spouse. We have our parents, in-laws, and kids forming our family lives. We have relatives and friends forming our social lives. If someone is careful about all four aspects of their life, then they can be called a successful individual.

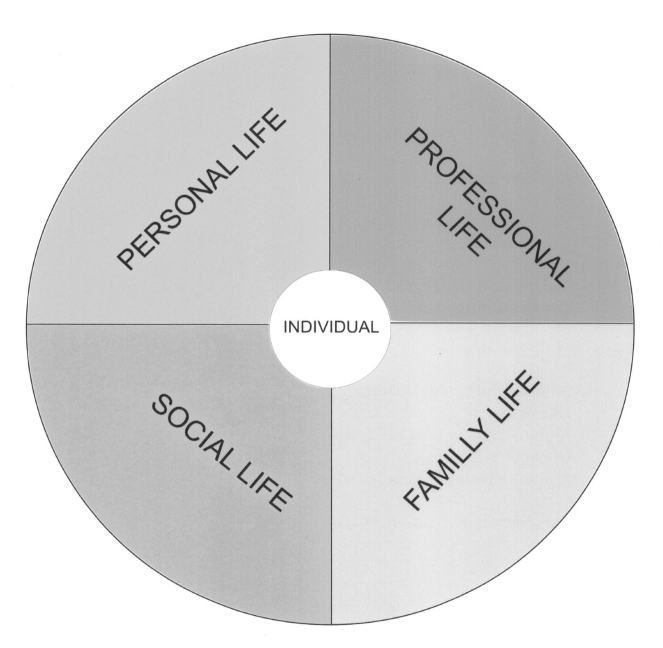

*We as individuals.*

Only a successful individual can clearly analyze his/her mind. The mind has three different parts. First of all, emotions; secondly, intelligence and finally, pride. Three of them function as a sail, oar, and rudder of a boat. A person who has control over these three behaves very differently than others!

If we categorize our daily conversation, then we find that our minds are in different stages.

1. Non-communal discussion of the future about science, technology, economics etc.
2. Non-communal discussion of the past about history, literature, individual sports etc.
3. Discussion of ourselves.
4. Communal discussion about the past.
5. Communal discussion about the future.

Finally, we can observe that.

1. An honest individual follows their responsibility over personal gain or loss.
2. An honest individual never discloses their mind to someone whom they do not trust.
3. A wise individual is never shocked in any situation.

In conclusion, an honest, intelligent, wise individual who investigates their mind can realize their true self.

# ABOUT THE AUTHOR

Mr. Bishnubrata Patra studied M.Sc. in Physics at the University of Calcutta, India (2009). Later, he did his PhD in Bioengineering and Biophotonics at National Yang-Ming University, Taiwan (2014). He finished his first postdoctoral fellowship at Polytechnique Montreal, Canada. He was a research fellow at the Department of Chemistry, University of Southampton, UK (2017-2021). Along with their career, his hobby is reading history, politics, and philosophy.

Ingram Content Group UK Ltd.
Milton Keynes UK
UKHW050613190723
425387UK00002B/4